"America has no noble ruins, for the old houses are torn down to make way for the new. But, fortunately, some of the old barns still remain--the only structures that are allowed the dignity of pleasing decay."
~Eric Sloane, An Age of Barns

THE MATANUSKA COLONY BARNS • HELEN HEGENER • NORTHERN LIGHT MEDIA

"The barn was pleasantly warm in the winter when the animals spent most of their time indoors, and it was pleasantly cool in the summer when the big doors stood wide open to the breeze... It was the kind of barn that swallows like to build their nests in. It was the kind of barn that children like to play in." E.B. White, Charlotte's Web

THE MATANUSKA COLONY
Barns

Helen Hegener

Introduction by James H. Fox

Foreword by Barbara L. Hecker

with photographs by Eric Vercammen, Albert Marquez,
and many contributing photographers

NORTHERN LIGHT MEDIA

THE MATANUSKA COLONY BARNS

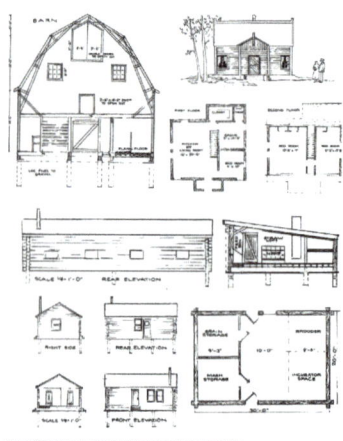

NORTHERN LIGHT MEDIA BOOKS

Post Office Box 298023
Wasilla, Alaska 99629
http://northernlightmedia.com

© 2013 Northern Light Media

Front cover photograph: The Earl Wineck barn at the Alaska state fairgrounds, September, 2012. Photo by Helen Hegener/Northern Light Media.
Frontispiece photo: Glendon Doughty barn on McLeod Road, by Susan Patch.
Photograph page 3: George Venne barn, by Eric Vercammen/Northern Light Media.
Back cover photograph (small): Ferber Bailey barn, by Helen Hegener/Northern Light Media.
Opposite page: Sjodin barn, original graphic by Susan Patch.

Photographers: Helen Hegener, Eric Vercammen, Albert Marquez, Joanie Juster, Barbara Hecker, and Susan Patch. Additional photographs by Stewart Amgwert and Ron Day, and from the collections of Jim Fox, Dave Rose, Glen Archer, Margaret Heaven, Kelley Griffin, and Kathy Laing. Photograph editing: Billy L. Fikes/Raven Graphics, and Albert Marquez/Planet Earth Adventures.

Historic photographs are used with permission from the Alaska State Library Archive Collections, Alaska Rural Rehabilitation Corporation., Mary Nan Gamble Collection, Willis T. Geisman, photographer; and from the University of Alaska, Fairbanks. The author is deeply grateful to all.

Introduction and "The Matanuska Colony Barns" ©2013 by James H. Fox. All rights reserved.

Copyright under International and Universal Copyright Conventions. All rights reserved. No part of this book may be reproduced or transmitted in any form or by any means, electronic or mechanical, including photocopying, recording, or by any information storage and retrieval system, without written permission from the copyright holder. Brief passages may be quoted for reviews of this book, and for third party advertising and promotional purposes only.

Hegener, Helen
   The Matanuska Colony Barns / Helen Hegener
   ISBN 978-0-9843977-4-7 (ISBN-10 0-9843977-4-4)
   1. Alaska History. 2. Palmer (Alaska)~History~Pictorial works.
   Includes appendixes: maps, bibliography, resources, indexes.

To order single copies of this book please send $34.00 (includes shipping) to the publisher:
Northern Light Media, PO Box 298023, Wasilla, Alaska 99629
Please make PayPal payments to helenhegener@gmail.com
Also available at Amazon, eBay, and wherever good books are sold. Whenever possible, please support the booksellers by ordering through your local independent bookstore.

Wholesale orders welcome, bulk orders and special purchases available. Contact us for details.

Northern Light Media publishes books about the history of Alaska. Other titles include *Along Alaskan Trails, The All Alaska Sweepstakes, Yukon Quest Album, The Stained Glass Dogteam, Long Hard Trails*, and the DVD *Appetite and Attitude: A Conversation with Lance Mackey*.

http://northernlightmedia.com   "Northern Light is different..."

THE MATANUSKA COLONY BARNS

As always, this book is for my children:
John, Jim, Jody, Chris, and Michael.
Once upon a time, when you were small,
we lived in a beautiful barn....

THE MATANUSKA COLONY BARNS

"Barns symbolize endurance, security, and stability, and they evoke a romanticized way of life. They remind us of our agrarian past, of less complicated times." -Charles Leik

The Parks and Archer Colony barns, combined as one. (Photo by Albert Marquez/Planet Earth Adventures)

CONTENTS

- **PART ONE - THE INSPIRATION**
  - Dedication 5
  - Preface, by Helen Hegener 9
  - Acknowledgements 10
  - Foreword, by Barbara L. Hecker 11
  - Introduction, by James H. Fox 12

- **PART TWO - THE CONTEXT**
  - The Matanuska Valley 17
  - A Brief History of Alaskan Barns 23
  - Before the Colonists Arrived 34
  - The Matanuska Colony Project 43
  - The Matanuska Colony Barns, by James H. Fox 51
  - The Legacy of the Colony Barns 55

- **PART THREE - THE BARNS**
  - Bailey/Estelle 65
  - Wilson/Larsh/Linn/Breeden/MATI 69
  - Puhl/Wilson/Miller/Bacon 73
  - Loyer/Lake 77
  - Havemeister 80
  - Anderson/Vickaryous/Roach/Luster/Bradley/Stevenson 83
  - Johnson/McCombs/Heaven 84
  - Lentz/Musk Ox Farm 88
  - Wineck/Alaska State Fair 91
  - Parks/Archer 96
  - Arndt/Swift 101
  - Monroe/Roark 102
  - Rebarchek/Mattson/Keyes 105
  - Sjodin/Klem/Sojka 107
  - Ising/Dragseth/Venne/Grover 108
  - Patten/Gorman 112
  - Barry/Hecker/Gardner 114
  - Stahler/Jensen/Bouwens/McCormick/Olson 118
  - Barns Album 120-127

- **PART FOUR - THE APPENDIXES**
  - Colonist Families 130
  - Colony Tract Maps 131-135
  - Bibliography & Resources 136-137
  - Barns Index & Locations Map 138
  - Index 139

THE MATANUSKA COLONY BARNS

"The Barns Are Always There"

Preface by Helen Hegener

Left: A local landmark, the Havemeister barn on Bogard Road. Above: Wagon wheels stored in a barn on Leroi and Margaret Heaven's farm. (Both by Helen Hegener/Northern Light Media) *Facing page: The George Venne barn on the Wes Grover farm, Grover Lane, Palmer.* (Albert Marquez/Planet Earth Adventures)

It has been my good fortune to live in and near the Matanuska Valley for more than 40 years, and the Matanuska Colony barns have always been a part of my life in Alaska. Driving the roads around Palmer and Wasilla, one sees the old structures often, glimpsed down a tree-lined dirt lane or silhouetted sharply against a mountain backdrop, and they rarely fail to bring a smile. Like trusted and comforting old friends, the barns are always there.

These old Colony barns evoke many pleasant memories for me, like the smell of horses and the creak of leather in the huge Linn-Breeden barn at the old Matanuska Stables, where my friend Margaret Heaven and I whiled away many summer days after our long morning rides. I remember working long, hot dusty afternoons to salvage beautiful lumber from a collapsed Colony barn when my husband and I were building our first home on Fairview Loop Road; and many years later I played hide-and-seek with my young sons in an old abandoned Colony barn which has long since disappeared.

I loved shopping for fresh fruits and vegetables at an old Colony barn turned into a roadside market, and I have enjoyed many interesting exhibits at the restored Wineck Barn at the Alaska State Fairgrounds. When our family needed a place to board our four horses we met Wes Grover, who owns a few hundred acres of beautiful woods and pastures on the Matanuska River, and not just one or two, but *three* Colony barns, and we loved riding our horses along the river not far from soaring Pioneer Peak.

I've been living with, admiring, and casually photographing these picturesque barns for over four decades, and in that time I've asked many questions about them, which have mostly gone unanswered. This book is my attempt to find answers to some of those questions. ~•~

Acknowledgements

Left: Two Colony barns on the Wes Grover farm, south of Palmer. Above: Old milk cans in the old Ralph Bradley barn, on the Leroi and Margaret Heaven farm. (Helen Hegener/Northern Light Media)

As I researched the historic 1935 Matanuska Colony Project and learned about the barns which were part and parcel of the plan, I was fortunate to meet and become friends with many people whose knowledge of, experience with, and enthusiasm for these beautiful structures resonated with my work. I am very thankful to everyone who took the time and made the effort to help me in telling the story of these magnificent Colony barns.

I am deeply grateful to Matanuska Valley historian James H. Fox, author of *The First Summer* (ARRC, 1980), whose encyclopedic knowledge of Colony history is an Alaskan treasure.

I am greatly indebted to my friend, filmmaker Joanie Juster, co-producer of the Colony documentary, *Alaska Far Away*, for opening doors for me which I didn't even know were there.

And I am forever grateful to my friend and partner Eric Vercammen, who believed in the Colony barns project from the beginning, and whose many beautiful barn photographs form the core of this book.

I am also thankful for these people who helped, in many large and small ways, to bring this book to reality:

- Arnold R. Alanen
- Stewart Amgwert
- Glen Archer
- Wayne Bouwens
- Theresa Daily
- Ron Day
- James and Krista Fee
- John and Annette Fee
- Billy Fikes
- Rhoda Friend
- Kelley Griffin
- Wes and Bonnie Grover
- Margaret Heaven
- Barbara Hecker
- Linda Henning
- Robert Hoskins
- Sherry Jackson
- Hugh A. Johnson
- Lorie Kirker
- Jean Krupa
- Kathy (Roark) Laing
- Rita and Dottie Loyer
- Murray Lundberg
- Albert Marquez
- Colleen Mielke
- Susan Patch
- June Price
- Heather Resz
- Dave and Diane Rose
- Lynn Sandvik
- Fran Seager-Boss
- Maureen Stevenson
- Earl and Ruth Wineck

A Note on Future Editions

Those who know the history of the Matanuska Colony Project and are familiar with the barns will recognize there are many not included in this book. I view this as the culmination of only the first year of what will undoubtedly be a multi-year research project on the barns, and as the research progresses, so too will this book progress, and new editions, larger and more comprehensive, will be published. If you have photographs, stories, family histories, or if you own a Colony barn or two, I hope you'll get in touch with me through my website:

http://matanuskabarns.wordpress.com

~Helen Hegener

Foreword • by Barbara L. Hecker

My family's big red Colony barn was my first cathedral, arching heavenward, mimicking the embracing mountains. It served as both playground and workplace. I knew where the barn cats hid their newborn litters. Calves were my pets and playmates. I sprawled undetected (or so I thought), reading my stash of books, soaking in both sun and sunset. I recall my Dad, perched on a short stool, head firmly pressed into the cow's flank, two-handedly, rapidly, rhythmically squeezing shot after shot of foamy milk into a metal bucket - and sometimes, just for giggles, into cats' begging maws. Once the Grade-A milking parlor was built, the old Colony barn was converted to calf pens. Mucking those pens was a frequent chore, as well as distributing daily water, grain and hay. I learned responsibility and ethics in that barn. Regardless the season or the reason, young cows require attention.

Once, playing with matches and straw, I almost burned down the barn. The trauma of blinding smoke, of evacuating terrified, balking animals, of fire engines screaming into the yard, provided sufficient lesson that no further punishment was mentioned. Fortunately, bits of singed wood and burnt straw were all the barn suffered.

I first met Helen Hegener while gathering information for a *Frontiersman* article on the 2012 restoration of 'my' Colony barn. The farm, farmhouse and barn had been out of my family's ownership since 1989. Still standing tall, the barn showed the wear and wobble of seventy-seven winters and innumerable, merciless Matanuska winds. Without intervention, it would not have withstood many more.

With Helen's presentation, my concept of the barn morphed from nostalgic to consciousness of its fraternity with other barns throughout the valley. My appreciation grew for the original design and the transient workers allocated to build the barn in 1935. I was awed by the obvious maintenance, upgrades, and back-breaking expense put into the barn during my Dad's 45-year guardianship. My gratitude deepened for Dr. Vaughn and Karen Gardner's care and dedication to what is now a renovated beauty, original logs revealed, with walls and floors straight and fortified, sporting fresh paint, bright red and white doors, and a new steel roof.

Helen brought to the fore what my mind's eye had painted as background - other Colony family stories, other Colony barns. I'd spotted most. I'd played in a few. I'd sadly watched too many consumed by harsh, bullying winds. Others were razed in favor of new barns, or, regrettably, subdivisions. Numerous Colony barns - in disrepair, unkempt and unloved - are readying to disappear forever from our Matanuska Valley landscape.

Helen's book on the Matanuska Colony Barns brings education, loving awareness and essential attention to the status of our remaining Matanuska barns. She provides names, story, and sense of place to each barn. Helen's work chronicles these simple, lovely, remarkable structures that symbolize, more than any other, the ambitious agricultural experiment that was the Matanuska Colony.

Barbara L. Hecker, Palmer, Alaska
Retired Educator, Freelance Writer

The barn built for the Earl Barry family in 1936, on Colony tract number 140, was purchased by Barbara Hecker's grandparents, Earl and Kathreen Hecker, in the early 1940's. In 1948 Barbara's parents, William and Bergie Hecker, took over the farm and turned it into a Grade A dairy. (Photos courtesy of Barbara L. Hecker)

Introduction • by James H. Fox

Three Scott Road barns in their prime: Ring/McCallister (left); Benson (center); and Beylund (right) circa 1949, north and west of Palmer. Henning Benson planting potatoes. (photo courtesy James H. Fox)

Helen Hegener has written a sensible, informative history of the Colony barns. By selecting various barns familiar to residents and visitors of the Valley, she has told the story of one settlement in a new way. It is a factual book, not sentimental in any way, yet it will evoke many sentiments and memories for those of us who grew up with, worked in, or drove past these barns over the years. Relics of a time long gone.

My grandparents, Henning and Irene Benson, were Colonists. As a young boy, their big barn was a wonderful, mysterious, and magical place for me. I had free reign of it: At age two or three watching my grandmother take new piglets into the house from an old sow with little maternal instinct; climbing up the wooden stairs behind a wooden door to the haymow full of dust motes electric in the shafts of light, dancing to the cooing of pigeons who were nesting between the side wall studs, descendants of homesteader John Bugge's flock that used to live in his old log barn; a rowboat on its side - disappearing as the haymow filled with hay from summer and autumn harvests, reappearing in spring as the hay diminished.

The granary - a ground floor room beside the stairs - held a smaller tin room, rodent-proofed to protect the feed grain and spring seed. Horse collars, reins, and tack hung on the walls, which my grandfather first used during his second summer in Alaska, in 1936, until he bought a tractor at the end of WW II.

In the main, south half of the barn were metal stanchions from end-to-end above a concrete floor put in by grandpa as he worked to upgrade the barn to a Grade A dairy before his sudden death in 1950. On the interior white-washed wall opposite the stanchions were the names of cows in his hand, along with the amount of milk they gave, when they'd freshened, been bred, and the date of their calves' births. A bovine history and genealogy in pencil, still there.

I visited other barns as a child, all with a unique scent of fresh as well as aged manures from cows, chickens, horses, pigs, and pigeons - the same warm earthy smells I find in most farm-made cheeses today - what the vintners in France refer to as *terroir*. Each barn had its own *terroir* from the animals, the feeds and hays, the soaps and disinfectants used to clean the milk rooms, and from constant use and disuse over the years.

I would always be in the barn when I spent any time at my grandmother's. From the age of eight I helped her with chores on occasion, but mostly with the haying, still done using horse drawn equipment pulled by a 1946 Farmall-A tractor. I pitched hay to the back of the mow as she tossed it in loose through the little pony-wall hay door above the main doors, tromping it down, loving the dry green smell of fast sun-dried hay. When rain fell on drying hay it became musty. I could tell how many times the hay had been wet or how fast it had dried by its smell. If it was still slightly moist we would sprinkle it with salt from the feed store to keep it from fermenting or igniting. A wooden barn filled 10-12' high with dry hay was a joy, a job well done, and a tremendous fire hazard.

Fire never harmed our barn. It was one winter when we had stronger than normal winds. The big haymow door hadn't been shut. A slight sag in the corner of the ground floor walls that summer had loosened the two levels of the barn. Together these allowed the winds to sweep in through the big door, pull the entire upper part of the barn off the lower portion, lifting and moving it ten feet or so, sitting it back down on the back southwest corner like a cocked hat. It wasn't possible to restore: the top was demolished. A small gable roof was built over the haymow floor, which is how it stands today, all slowly sinking into the ground.

My grandmother continued to raise and milk cows in the lower part of the barn. In the fiercest winter winds, morning and night she milked. Sometimes I would help after school, carrying buckets of warm water from the house, through the howling winds, over snowdrifts twice my height, and down steps carved into them, struggling to pull open the doors to carry in the diminished water supply, and becoming enveloped in the sweet smells of hay, cows, cow urine, and the earthy fresh manure mixed with bedding hay that had to be forked out and replaced.

The body heat from the cows warmed the barns. It was still inside with the door closed against the howling wind. Cats joined us as we fed, watered, and cleaned the cows' stalls. Then my grandmother pulled a stool up to the rear side of a cow, sat, washed the udder clean, tucked her head into the cleft between Blacky's, Lazy's, Granny's or Ugly's back leg and stomach, and began pulling on the teats. The sharp, tinny, musical sound of milk hitting the pail would draw the cats near. Once in a while they were rewarded when grandma would aim a teat at a cat and strip out a stream of warm milk to its face or into its mouth, grandma giggling like a little girl as the cats jumped towards streams aimed above them. The cow would munch slowly and deliberately on the hay, chewing its cud, occasionally looking back to see that the hands still belonged to their friend. My grandmother treated her cows so well they were spoiled and wouldn't let their milk down for anyone but her.

I loved those times of quiet communion between her and the animals. It was a natural world where each species lived in harmony, respect, and what can only be called a family. Such a communion of interspecies still exists in some parts of the world today, but too many of us have lost it - or never had the opportunity to be a member of it.

Helen has brought back those memories for me; and perhaps she can give those of you reading this book an idea of why these barns are so important. Today they stand as obvious symbols of the farming and dairy past of this Valley. They are also reminders of a time when people worked for themselves, when life seemed simple, was difficult, full of hard work and simple fun. It was also a time when man and animals spoke to each other and respected each other in an unsentimental natural world, full of life and of death.   ~•~

THE MATANUSKA COLONY BARNS

ABOVE: KERTTULA BARN BY STEWART AMGWERT. RIGHT: VANDERWEELE-KEYES BARN BY ALBERT MARQUEZ.

THE MATANUSKA COLONY BARNS

PART ONE - THE CONTEXT

THE MATANUSKA COLONY BARNS

The Matanuska Valley

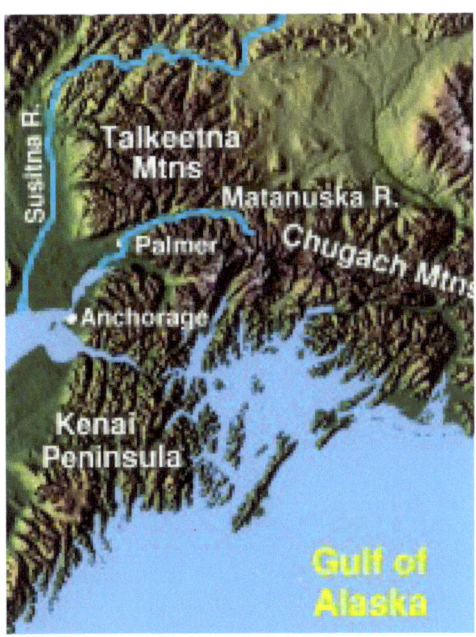

Left: Aerial view of Colony Farms on the Springer System south of Palmer (ARRC photo, University of Alaska Fairbanks). Facing page: Pioneer Peak as viewed from Bodenburg Loop Road. (Helen Hegener/Northern Light Media) *Above: Portion of a map of southcentral Alaska showing Palmer and the Matanuska River* (copyright 2004 by Matthew Trump, from the Wikimedia Commons)

Namesake of the Valley

The Matanuska Valley is situated at the headwaters of Knik Arm, a branching of southcentral Alaska's Cook Inlet, which further branches into the Matanuska and Knik Rivers. The Matanuska River, namesake of the valley, begins 75 miles away in the Chugach Mountains, flowing from under the 27-mile long glacier of the same name. The river delineates the Chugach range to the south and the Talkeetna Mountains to the north.

The Knik River tumbles out of the 25-mile-long Knik Glacier, another of the largest glaciers in southcentral Alaska, and flows down the broad Knik River Valley, With a name derived from a Dena'ina word, it rolls along under the towering Pioneer Peak, a well-known landmark and part of the Chugach mountain range. The peak, located only nine miles south of Palmer, rises 6,398' from sea level, and dominates the southern skyline from almost every part of the eastern side of the Matanuska Valley.

Both the Knik and Matanuska glaciers are the remnants of a massive icefield which once filled the valley to a depth of several thousand feet. The glacier's slow retreat from the valley left the land pockmarked with large and small lakes, hollows, ridges, and rock outcroppings, including the 881-foot-high Bodenburg Butte, a prominent local landmark just south and east of the Matanuska River.

The Mountains Dominate

Mountains are ever-present in the Matanuska Valley, from the soaring peaks of the Chugach Range to the south and east, to the less rugged but no less daunting ridges of the Talkeetna Mountains to the north, there are few places in the valley where the mountains are not in view. Even to the west, while mostly open due to the vast expanses of the Susitna River Valley, there's the long silhouette of the picturesque Mt. Susitna, known

"The mountains are close by..."

locally as the Sleeping Lady, and on clear days the Alaska Range is in view, with Mt. Foraker, Mt. Hunter, and the great Denali itself often on the horizon.

In his book *The Frontier in Alaska and the Matanuska Colony*, Orlando W. Miller describes the somewhat daunting terrain: "The whole valley... was not an unbroken expanse of good agricultural land, and the word valley rather misleadingly suggests a greater regularity than one would find there. At the eastern end, at Matanuska Junction or Palmer, the mountains dominate three-quarters of the horizon, the Talkeetnas to the north and the Chugach to the east and south, rising so sharply just beyond the Matanuska River that their shadow affects the local climate, reducing the period of spring daylight and delaying plant growth."

The mountains are close by, to be sure, and there are not many inroads offering access to them. For the most part they define and delineate a wild boundary which even today scant few people cross for any reason other than hunting or recreation.

Palmer Hay Flats

The tremendous glaciers which shaped and formed the Matanuska Valley left behind hundreds of lakes and ponds, a delight for canoe and kayak paddlers, and most of the lakes are kept well stocked for fishermen. Several creeks tumble down out of the mountains to meander across the valley. There are large forests of birch mixed with white spruce in the well-drained areas, while dwarf stick-like black spruce stand in the poorly drained swampy lowlands.

One of the most significant features of the area is the thousands of acres comprising the Palmer Hay Flats, once natural hayfields, now a coastal and freshwater wetland area which includes tidal sloughs and mudflats, lakes and streams, and upland birch forests. It is an important stop for thousands of migratory birds, and an equally important winter range for the valley's hundreds of resident moose.

Left: A lake north and west of Palmer, with the Talkeetna Mountains in the background. (Helen Hegener/Northern Light Media)

THE MATANUSKA COLONY BARNS

The Matanuska River east of Palmer, and the Chugach Mountains. (Photo by Helen Hegener/Northern Light Media)

THE MATANUSKA COLONY BARNS

"A recreational paradise..."

Left: Pioneer Peak across the Palmer hayflats. The town of Matanuska was in the trees near the right-hand side of this photo. Above: The Matanuska River with Bodenburg Butte rising in the center of the photo, and the Chugach Mountains dropping off to Eklutna on the right, taken from Clark-Wolverine Road, east of Palmer. (Both: Helen Hegener/Northern Light Media)

Breadbasket of the State

The Matanuska Valley's natural attractions have made it a recreational paradise, with lakes for fishing, boating, and swimming; rivers for fishing and white-water rafting; endless trails for hiking, backpacking, and horseback riding. There are many miles of bicycle pathways in the valley, extensive multi-use trails for both snowmachines and sled dog travel, and back-country roads for exploring and four-wheel driving fun.

In the 2012 *Alaska Visitor's Guide*, writer Melissa DeVaughn refers to the Matanuska Valley as "the breadbasket of the state, dotted with picturesque barns surrounded by fields of green."

She continues, "Today the valley, composed of Palmer and the nearby community of Wasilla, has a heartland-U.S.A. vibe. The rich soil generates some of the state's best produce and much of it can be enjoyed at local eateries and farmer's markets."

Vibrant Past, Bright Future

The Matanuska Valley's complex, colorful and vibrant past has left it speckled with picturesque farms and fields which stand in stark contrast to the wilderness only a few miles away. At the same time, the rampant growth of the Matanuska Valley's population and the incessant subdivision and development of what was once rich farmland threatens those picturesque elements, even as heritage-aware groups form and fight to save the farms and historic buildings which remain. ~•~

"Back in 1935, those original Valley Colonists already knew this fertile valley could produce a rich agrarian heritage, making Palmer the only Alaskan community to develop from an agricultural lifestyle."
-City of Palmer website

THE MATANUSKA COLONY BARNS

THE MATANUSKA COLONY BARNS

22

THE MATANUSKA COLONY BARNS

A Brief History of Alaskan Barns

Left and above: James Taylor Dog Barn, Yukon River, Opposite 4th of July Creek, Eagle (Library of Congress, Prints & Photographs Division, HABS AK 19-EGL.V, 3-B--1) **Opposite page: Government Farm near Fairbanks, 1916.** (Library of Congress, HABS LC-DIG-ppmsc-02210)

The Yukon: Dog Barns

The first shelters for animals in Alaska were likely the small crudely-built trail barns for the passenger, freight, and mail dogteams which traveled the winter trails. When staying in one place for a length of time, dog drivers would construct rough canvas tents for their teams, and many owners built dog barns to house their weary dogs in more comfort at home. In *Buildings of Alaska*, Alison Hoagland describes a dog barn built by James Taylor, "a miner turned trapper who built himself an intricate set of buildings on the north side of the Yukon River, probably in about 1924."

Hoagland detailed the dog barn Taylor built for his team: "The dog barn, a low cabin with saddle-notched log walls, has six stalls with vertical-pole walls. Each stall has its own door, operable by an outside lever. Taylor also built individual doghouses out of logs and extensive vertical-pole corrals that led down to a stream."

Not far from James Taylor's dog barn, also on the Yukon River, one of the most impressive kennels in Alaska was built at the direction of then-Lieutenant William "Billy" Mitchell, who was at that time charged with building an extensive network of telegraph and cable lines that would link Alaska to the rest of the world. The Washington-Alaska Military Cable and Telegraph System (WAMCATS) would connect Fort Liscum in Valdez to other forts along the Yukon River: Fort Egbert at Eagle City, Fort Gibbon at Tanana, and St. Michael on the Bering Sea coast.

To accomplish this mission, Billy Mitchell, who would later gain a Major General's stars and earn fame and controversy as the "father of the U.S. Air Force," bought 80 huskies, 40 sets of harnesses and 16 sleds, an unprecedented investment. To house the huskies Mitchell had 19 sled dog kennels added to the south side of the

THE MATANUSKA COLONY BARNS

"The hay loft was built in 1901..."

Left: Dogsleds in hay loft, Fort Egbert mule barn, Eagle. (Library of Congress, Prints & Photographs Division, HABS AK19-EGL.V,1-A--10) **Above: Mule stalls with names.** (Library of Congress, Prints & Photographs Division, HABS AK19-EGL.V, 1-A--8) **Right: Dog kennels at the Ft. Egbert mule barn, Eagle.** (Library of Congress, Prints & Photographs Division, HABS AK V, 1-A--3)

mule barn. In June, 1903, Lt. Mitchell's crews completed construction of the first telegraph line to span the interior of Alaska.

According to the booklet *Eagle-Fort Egbert: A Remnant of the Past*, produced through the cooperative efforts of the Bureau of Land Management and the Eagle Historical Society & Museums, the first floor of the mule barn, or quartermaster stables, was completed prior to May 1900 at a cost of $550 for materials. It housed 53 animals. Some of the mules' names hang above the stall doors. The hay loft was built in 1901. The barn was used until 1911. Today it contains exhibits from the past: a blacksmith area, sickbay stall, mule harnesses and hardware, old wagons, mining and agriculture memorabilia, boats and dog sleds.

Nenana: Substantial Buildings

The name Nenana means "a good place to camp between the rivers," and before that name it was known as Toghotthele, which means, "the hill next to the river." According to Alison K. Hoagland's *Buildings of Alaska*: "At the turn of the twentieth century, Nenana was an Athapaskan Indian village. James Duke set up a trading post here in 1903, and Nenana's history would have been unexceptional if it had not been for the Alaska Railroad. With a strategic location at the confluence of the Tanana and Nenana rivers, Nenana was originally intended as a construction camp where materials to build the railroad to the south could be unloaded from steamboats. The Alaska Engineering Commission built some substantial buildings..."

Among those "substantial buildings," which included dormitories, a cafeteria, a hospital and others, was the A.E.C. stable and barn, a two-story log-and-frame structure known as the Headquarters Barn and Stables. Unfortunately, like almost all of the A.E.C. buildings, it no longer

THE MATANUSKA COLONY BARNS

THE MATANUSKA COLONY BARNS

Archives, University of Alaska, Fairbanks

THE MATANUSKA COLONY BARNS

"A town straight out of a Mark Twain novel..."

Above: Creamer's Field barn in Fairbanks. (Photographer- Harper) Facing page: A.E.C. (Alaska Engineering Commission) stable and barn in Nenana, June 27, 1917. Signs above the door read "No Smoking" and "Barn No. 1". Caption reads: "No. 53. A. J. Johnson, Official photographer, A. E. C." (Albert Johnson Collection, 1905-1917 UAF-1989-166-626 University of Alaska Fairbanks)

survives, and photos of the huge and historic building are rare.

Nenana is once again a quiet place, described by one author as "...a town straight out of a Mark Twain novel: a sleepy, dusty riverside barge stop. Riverboats, in fact, still load with cargo for villages up and down the nearby Tanana River."

Fairbanks: Creamer's Dairy

Shortly after the turn of the century, Charles Hinckley and his wife Belle brought three cows and some horses up the Yukon and Tanana Rivers by sternwheeler, and they started a dairy to serve the gold-rich outpost of Fairbanks. In 1928, the Hinckleys sold the dairy to Charles and Anna Creamer; Charles was the son of close friends living nearby, and Anna was Belle Hinckley's younger sister.

The new owners named the farm Creamer's Dairy, and during the 1930s and 1940s, the Creamers worked hard to modernize and expand the business. They built two large Louden barns, designed by the Louden Machinery Co. of Iowa, which still give Creamer's its distinctive visual appeal. The larger barn cost $13,700, more than the entire dairy had been worth ten years earlier. The hayloft held 165 tons of hay, enough to feed 55 cows through the winter. In 1938 the Creamers threw a huge dance and invited the whole town to celebrate the opening of the new barn and its state-of-the-art equipment. According to a report in the News-Miner the next day, nearly everyone in Fairbanks attended.

The dairy thrived throughout the next few decades, and when it finally ceased production in 1966 it was the largest and most successful dairy in Interior Alaska. The town of Fairbanks lobbied the state to purchase the entire dairy and 1,800 acres of land, which has since become the popular Creamer's Field Migratory Waterfowl Refuge, under the supervision of the

THE MATANUSKA COLONY BARNS

The Matanuska Experiment Station above (image no. UAF1968000400821) and the photos on the following pages, are from the Agricultural Experiment Station Photograph Collection Albums; 23 albums documenting the work done on the experimental farms and stations between 1913 and 1959, and containing photographs, film, reports, correspondence, pamphlets, and administrative records received from the agricultural stations at Matanuska, Fairbanks, and Petersburg. The papers address topics such as environmental data, Alaskan flora, dairy projects, grazing lands, and fur farming.
(Agricultural Experiment Station Photograph Collection, Alaska and Polar Regions Collections, University of Alaska Fairbanks)

Alaska Department of Fish and Game. The structures are the only surviving pioneer dairy buildings in Interior Alaska, and in 1977 they were admitted to the National Register of Historic Places.

Science-Based Farm Research

In most parts of Alaska barns were few and far between, but as the land grew more settled, more barns were built to shelter valuable livestock and equipment, and to store feed.

The Hatch Act of 1887 authorized agricultural experiment stations in the United States and its territories to provide science-based research information to farmers. In 1898 the federal government established the first Alaska Agricultural Experiment Stations in Sitka and Kodiak, and stations in Kenai, Rampart, Copper Center, and Fairbanks followed quickly.

In 1917 the Alaska Agricultural Experiment Station was established at Matanuska when M.D. Snodgrass selected 240 acres for the site on the recommendation of the Alaska Engineering Commission. In 1923, at a meeting at the farm, the Matanuska Valley Settlers Association was created to reduce freight shipping rates to the Valley.

In 1931 the federal government transferred ownership of all experiment station facilities to the College of Agriculture and Mines in Fairbanks, which was renamed the University of Alaska in 1935. As population centers shifted, goals and objectives for agricultural research changed and the stations at Copper Center, Kenai, Rampart, Kodiak, and Sitka were closed. ~•~

"There are many persons who are happier in a simple existence, living largely through their own efforts in a self-sufficient way... We had it once in America, and there are those who feel we lost something valuable in our departure from it..."
-Rexford G. Tugwell, agricultural economist for Roosevelt's New Deal

THE MATANUSKA COLONY BARNS

"Barns were few and far between..."

(Archives, University of Alaska Fairbanks, Agricultural Experiment Station Photograph Collection, Image no. uaf1968000400934)

THE MATANUSKA COLONY BARNS

Barn at the Matanuska Experiment Station. (Archives, University of Alaska Fairbanks, Agricultural Experiment Station Photograph Collection, Image no. uaf1968000400830a)

At the Matanuska Experiment Station. (Archives, University of Alaska Fairbanks, Agricultural Experiment Station Photograph Collection, Image no. uaf1968000400926)

THE MATANUSKA COLONY BARNS

Fairbanks Experiment Station. (Archives, University of Alaska Fairbanks, Agricultural Experiment Station Photograph Collection, Image no. uaf196800040075)

THE MATANUSKA COLONY BARNS

(Archives, University of Alaska Fairbanks, Agricultural Experiment Station Photograph Collection, Image no. uaf1968000400236)

THE MATANUSKA COLONY BARNS

Before the Colonists Arrived

Left: Dogteam hauling coal in front of George W. Palmer's store in Knik, 1909. Above: Palmer depot and section house, White's farm on the left, circa 1917. (Alaska Railways Photograph Album UAF-1996-0190-8 University of Alaska Fairbanks) **Right: G.H. Saindon's farm, 4 miles above Matanuska, 1917.** (Alaska Railways Photo Album UAF-1996-0190-2 University of Alaska Fairbanks)

Trail Comes Out River

George Palmer's trading station on the Matanuska River was established between 1894 and 1898 to take advantage of the trails between the Cook Inlet region and the Copper River area. According to Wikipedia: *"The indigenous Dena'ina Athabascan name for the river is Ch'atanhtnu, based on the root -tanh 'trail extends out', meaning literally 'trail comes out river'."*

In her small book titled *Old Times on Upper Cook's Inlet*, Louise Potter describes the early trails through the Valley: "...the Indians must have marked walking trails through the Upper Inlet country well before 1898 and, after that time, prospectors brushed-out trail after trail, both winter and summer, leading from the coast to the coal and gold mines. Many of these trails were later widened for the use of dog teams and for saddle and pack horses and sleds. Eventually, some even became the government mail routes and, today, are busy roads."

Louise Potter continues, "A map of the Inlet area, copyrighted in 1899, shows eight such 'Trails Used by Natives...'" and she describes the one which probably led to the name "trail comes out river": "A summer trail from old Knik up the Matanuska River, passing 'Palmer's Upper House' (store) and King's House to Millich Creek and, via Hick's Creek, Trail Lake, and Nulchuck Tyon Village, to the Copper River (pretty much the route of the present Glenn Highway)."

The Railroad: Gold and Coal

Gold mining and coal fields prompted construction of one or two roads into the Valley at or predating 1914, and providing food for the construction workers spurred clearing and planting of the first farmsteads in the area. Gold prospecting in the Valley reached its peak in 1919, and an increase in the value spiked activity between 1933 and the beginning of

THE MATANUSKA COLONY BARNS

Archives, University of Alaska, Fairbanks

THE MATANUSKA COLONY BARNS

THE MATANUSKA COLONY BARNS

"...nearly all the land had been homesteaded..."

Above: The Alaska Agricultural Experiment Station at Matanuska, founded in 1917 and still at this location (now on Trunk Road), date of photo unknown. (Charles E. Bunnell Collection UAF-1958-1026-1990 University of Alaska Fairbanks) *Facing page: J. Heady's homestead near Palmer, photo dated October 9, 1918.* (Photographer: H.G. Kaiser. Alaska Engineering Commission)

World War II. Interest in the coal fields was led by the U.S. Navy seeking a source of coal for refueling the Pacific Fleet without needing to return to the United States. In 1913, the USS Maryland conducted tests on 1,100 tons of bituminous coal from Chickaloon and found it to be quite satisfactory for Naval purposes, although it would not be utilized until the government railroad was constructed in 1917.

In *Matanuska Valley Memoir*, Bulletin #18 from the Alaska Experiment Station, July, 1955, authors Hugh A. Johnson and Keith L. Stanton describe early farming development:

"Agriculture in the Valley came into its own in 1915. Most of the 150 settlers filing for homesteads came intending to farm. Some cleared enough land to put in a crop the next year. Settlement was concentrated in the vicinity of Knik, across the Hay Flats and up the Matanuska River with a few homesteads spotted along the trails leading to Fishhook Creek. The greatest influx of settlers occurred in 1916 and 1917. By the end of that period nearly all the available land had been homesteaded, a fact not commonly known."

In *Old Times on Upper Cook's Inlet*, Louise Potter printed a list of 132 people who had homesteads adjacent to nearby Knik in 1915, noting, "That such a list is possible at all is apt to come as a surprise to many who have been encouraged to believe that 1935, the date the 'Colonists' arrived in the Matanuska Valley, marks the beginning of the history of agriculture in the Upper Inlet Region..."

It was the Colonists' good fortune to land in a dramatically beautiful valley which already had a rich and vibrant history, and they contributed hard work and dreams of a better future to help build it into a dynamic and vibrant place. But Alaska was being advertised and promoted to

THE MATANUSKA COLONY BARNS

"... the slanted light of the higher latitudes..."

Left: **Rudolph Weiss farm, two miles north of Matanuska Junction, circa 1914-1917** (Photographer: Phinney S. Hunt, Alaska Railways Photograph Album UAF-1996-0190-12 University of Alaska Fairbanks) Right: **"Joe Kircher's farmstead. Note earth roofs on house and barns." Circa 1930.** (Photo by Willis T. Geisman, Mary Nan Gamble Collection ASL-P270-705 Alaska State Library)

farmers for many years before the Colonists headed north.

In an article for the *Pacific Northwest Quarterly*, October, 1978, which was later reprinted in the anthology *Interpreting Alaska's History*, James R. Shortridge wrote about the many government and private efforts to promote Alaska as an agricultural Promised Land: "...almost every promoter lauded the long summer days and their amazing effect on vegetable quality and size. One enthusiast called the tropical sun 'too intense' for best plant growth whereas 'the slanted light of the higher latitudes is always soft and delicate, stimulating growth and not retarding it.' According to some, these magical conditions impart to Alaskan produce 'such superior flavor that when a person has once eaten the vegetables grown in Alaska, other vegetables are insipid and tasteless.'"

"Anchorage was only a village"

Joe Kircher and his family arrived in the Matanuska Valley in 1932 and purchased a 320 acre homestead on Wasilla Creek from Oliver Krough, the storekeeper in Matanuska. In the Spring, 1977 issue of *Touchstone Magazine* Joe wrote, "The greatest drawback in the development of the Valley in the early thirties was the lack of a market for the Valley produce. Anchorage was only a village of a little over 3000 population, depending on what time of year you took the census. All had their little gardens and there were three small dairies which took care of the fresh milk used. The people of Anchorage had an apathetic attitude toward buying Valley produce. Many thought farming in the Valley was impossible and that those who tried it were lacking in intelligence. This attitude changed when the colonists came. Of the four million dollars spent in the Valley, a good share of it went to Anchorage. Anchorage at that time needed a booster shot in her economy

THE MATANUSKA COLONY BARNS

Joe Kitchen farmstead. Note earth roofs on house and barn.

Alaska State Library - Historical Collections

THE MATANUSKA COLONY BARNS

Above: Barn at the Fairbanks Experimental Station (Archives, University of Alaska Fairbanks, Agricultural Experiment Station Photograph Collection, Image no. uaf196800040069) *Right: Looking east down the street in Anchorage now called Fourth Avenue, 1930-32.* (Walter W. Hodge Papers, ca. 1925-1948 UAF-2003-63-106 University of Alaska Fairbanks)

as much as the Valley and the outlook changed."

A Plan to Colonize and Develop

In 1935 the U.S. government devised a plan to colonize and develop a pioneering community in Alaska. According to *Matanuska Valley Memoir*, the Colony Project brought 202 midwest farm families to the valley in an unprecedented resettlement program "...established for three purposes: to take people off, or keep them off, relief as a result of the depression in the United States; to demonstrate whether or not Alaska provided a settlement frontier that could absorb excess population; and to add greater support of the Alaskan economy by production of more locally produced food which would lessen dependence on costly and vulnerable waterborne transportation."

The population center at Anchorage was ready to embrace the local production of farm goods, and the Agricultural Experiment Station was showing how fruitful the Matanuska Valley could be.

Still, as the authors of *Matanuska Valley Memoir* pointed out, the valley was not an untamed wilderness when the Colonists arrived: "It is not generally known that homesteads had owned most of the better lands in the Matanuska Valley for 20 years before the Colony was founded." ~•~

"Alaska's natural splendors are overwhelming. From the snow-covered peak of Mt. McKinley to the volcanic islands of the Aleutian chain, from the expansive treeless tundra of the North Slope to the tall spruce and deep fjords of Southeast, the nature of Alaska is wild, vast, and magnificent. Humans are diminutive by comparison, and their architecture equally so."
-Alison K. Hoagland, author, Buildings of Alaska

"Anchorage was ready to embrace local production..."

Archives, University of Alaska, Fairbanks

Colonists hauling logs to their cabin sites.
Alaska State Library - Historical Collections

The Matanuska Colony Project

Cabin construction
Alaska State Library - Historical Collections

Above: A friend talks to Margaret Nelson (on the right, with daughter Norma) upon their arrival at Matanuska (ASL-P270-225) *Left: Cabin construction* (ASL-P270-488) *Facing page: Colonists hauling logs to their cabin sites* (ASL-P270486) (All photos by Willis T. Geisman, Mary Nan Gamble Collection, Alaska State Library)

Roosevelt's Three R's

Anyone who travels through the eastern part of Alaska's dramatically beautiful Matanuska Valley soon finds a Colony barn enhancing the landscape. These striking Valley landmarks are the enduring legacy of an all-but-forgotten chapter in American history, when the U.S. government took a direct hand in the lives of thousands of its citizens, offering Depression-distraught farm families an opportunity to begin again in a far-off land with government financing and support. The Matanuska Colony Project was part of President Franklin Delano Roosevelt's New Deal, a series of economic programs designed to provide the "3 R's": Relief, Recovery, and Reform." Relief for the poor and the unemployed, Recovery of the economy to normal levels, and Reform of the financial system to prevent a repeat depression.

The decade of the 1930's profoundly altered the course of Alaska's history, as relationships changed between the citizens, the state, and the federal government, and rugged Alaskan individualism gave way to an acceptance of the government's increasing role in daily life. The Matanuska Colony was not the only government rural rehabilitation project; it was in fact only one of a multitude of complex, ambitious and controversial programs initiated under Franklin Roosevelt's New Deal Federal Rural Development Program, and other resettlement projects included Dyess Colony, Arkansas; Arthurdale, West Virginia; the Phoenix Homesteads in Arizona; and similar colonies in over a dozen other states.

In his 1968 book, *The Colorful Matanuska Valley*, author and General Manager of the Matanuska Colony Project, Don L. Irwin, explained, "On February 4, 1935, President Roosevelt, by Executive Order No. 6957,

THE MATANUSKA COLONY BARNS

"There was no doctor, nor were there hospital facilities..."

Above: D.F. Watson holding turnips grown in his garden (ASL-P270-697)

Left: Saindon farm with Colony tent and old homesteader hay barn, located aouth of Palmer (ASL-P270-735) (All photos on both pages by Willis T. Geisman, Mary Nan Gamble Collection, Alaska State Library)

withdrew an area of 8,000 acres in the Matanuska Valley from homestead entry. This area was supplemented by a March 13 withdrawal of 18,000 acres of grazing land. Both of these withdrawals were for the benefit of the Colony Project."

The areas withdrawn lay generally along both sides of the lower reaches of the Matanuska River in the eastern part of the valley. The land there ranged from rolling benches to flat and fertile bottomland well-suited to farming, needing only to be cleared and plowed to become productive. Irwin detailed the early days of the Matanuska Valley, noting, "There were approximately 100 miles of graded road in the Valley in the spring of 1935. Not more than 20 miles was gravel surfaced and none of it was paved. There was no road from the Valley into Anchorage."

203 Families were selected

Irwin went on to explain there was weekly freight and passenger service on the Alaska Railroad, but no more than 1,200 acres of land cleared of timber and under cultivation. "One married couple and three elderly bachelors comprised the population of Palmer. There was no doctor, nor were there hospital facilities in the Valley."

It was into this frontier atmosphere the U.S. government brought their recruited settlers. With thousands answering the call, 203 families were eventually selected and transported to Alaska from the northern tier states of Michigan, Minnesota, and Wisconsin, as it was supposed that residents of these states would be most familiar with the harsh climate to be found in Alaska. A news clip from the *Ironwood Daily Globe*, of Ironwood, Michigan, explained the selection process for the Alaska-bound group in an article from March, 1935, titled '*Families in Northern Counties Will Begin Migration to Alaska in April*':

THE MATANUSKA COLONY BARNS

Above; Johan Johnson (Michigan) puts in his time in the community garden at Camp 2 with a cultivator (ASL-P270-761)
Right: A typical farm scene in the Matanuska Farm Colony. Mrs. E.H. Huseby, colonist mother in the garden behind her tent home picking turnips. In the background can be seen the Huseby's cabin in construction and their cattle. (ASL-P270-754)

"Madison, March 19--(AP)--Modern pioneers, in the person of 67 northern Wisconsin families now on relief, will begin their exodus to a "new frontier" and a 'new life' in Alaska late in April.

"Arlie Mucks, president of the Wisconsin Rural Rehabilitation Corporation, announced that Wisconsin's quota of the 200 families which will seek to rehabilitate themselves under federal direction in the fertile Matanuska valley, will sail from Seattle, Wash., in May together with similar groups from northern Michigan and Minnesota.

"All qualifications have not been determined, Mucks said, but the eligible families must have been on relief for some time, their members must be healthy and they must have an agricultural background. The husband and wife must be between 35 and 40, and willing to settle in the new Utopia..

"Four hundred CCC men and members of transient camps on the Pacific coast are being sent to Palmer this month to clear the land, build roads and houses, as well as a creamery, school building and community hall.

"When the settlers arrive, each will be assigned 40 acres of land. In rehabilitating the families, the government intends to spend $3,000 on each group, and the 'pioneers' must agree to liquidate the government advance over 30 years."

Only one design

On May 23, 1935, the colonists drew slips of paper from a cardboard box to determine which 40 acre tracts they would be farming. Parcels could be exchanged if, for example, two families wanted to be located together. The government architect, David R. Williams, had designed five house plans for practical and serviceable structures which could be built of frame construction, logs, or a combination of both types of materials.

THE MATANUSKA COLONY BARNS

Harvesting oats.
Alaska State Library - Historical Collections

THE MATANUSKA COLONY BARNS

"The barns came in only one design..."

Above: Colonists' children playing (ASL-P270-641) **Left: Mail day in Palmer** (ASL-P270-573) **Facing page: Harvesting oats** (ASL-P270-769) (All photos by Willis T. Geisman, Mary Nan Gamble Collection, Alaska State Library)

The barns, however, came in only one design, as explained by Johnson and Stanton in *Matanuska Valley Memoir*: "Only one plan was available. Each was 32 feet square, 32 feet high and had a 'hip' roof. The walls were logs to 10 feet above the ground and then siding to the roof. All were built on small pilings of native spruce which soon rotted away.

"The colonists complained from the start that the barns were too small, inefficiently partitioned, drafty and poorly built. The criticisms were apparently justified. Dairymen going into Grade A production had to spend large sums to make their barns useable. Some families sold their outbuildings. Many others have abandoned their barns and have allowed them to rot away--a complete loss and temporary monuments to regimentation."

Bizarre Circumstances

Much has been written about the Matanuska Colony Project over the years, both applauding the effort and roundly condemning it. Perhaps the fairest assessment comes from--once again--Johnson and Stanton in *Matanuska Valley Memoir*: "The Matanuska Colony was developed during an emergency period and under bizarre circumstances. A national emergency relief program obviously was not the best vehicle for a settlement experiment. The experiment was conducted with nearly all the ingredients as unknowns. It was complicated by some administrative decisions and actions obstructive to smooth development. It may not have been a case of the blind leading the blind--although at times it seemed so."

The Great American Dream

Although fraught with inevitable bureaucratic entanglements, frustrating delays, and a variety of other distractions, the Matanuska Colony actually thrived for the most part, and nearly 200 families remained

THE MATANUSKA COLONY BARNS

"The Colony barn has become a beloved symbol..."

Left: Cabin No. 140, Earl Barry, Sr. (ASL-P270-322 Photo by Willis T. Geisman, Mary Nan Gamble Collection, Alaska State Library) **Above: Pippel Colony farm** (UAF2009000100029 University of Alaska Fairbanks) **Right: "An old settler's mule team is quite a contrast to the trim airplane in the background."** (ASL-P270-937 Willis T. Geisman, Mary Nan Gamble Collection, Alaska State Library)

to raise their families and make their permanent homes in Alaska. Highways were built, the wide Matanuska and Knik Rivers were bridged, and the town of Palmer became the center of commerce and society in the valley. By 1948, production from the Colony Project farms provided over half of the total Alaskan agricultural products sold.

An editorial in the November, 1972 *Agroborealis* magazine, published by the University of Alaska Fairbanks, beckoned those who would join Alaska's farming pioneers: "The great American dream! To be independent. To be completely self reliant and, if possible, self sufficient. Not necessarily to be rich, but to be one's own boss and beholden to no one. This is what brought our forefathers to this continent in the first place. This is the rainbow that led them over the Alleghenies, across the plains, and through the mountain passes to California and Oregon. This is the magnet that still draws people to Alaska."

In his classic book, *An Age of Barns*, artist and author Eric Sloane wrote, "America has no noble ruins, for the old houses are torn down to make way for the new. But, fortunately, some of the old barns still remain--the only structures that are allowed the dignity of pleasing decay."

Today the Matanuska Valley draws worldwide attention for its colorful agricultural heritage and its uniquely orchestrated history. The iconic Colony barn, often seen around the valley now in artwork, logos, advertising, and other uses, has become a beloved symbol of Alaskan history. ~•~

"It's part of the Palmer landscape to have the characteristic... barn."
-Fran Seager-Boss, Matanuska Susitna Borough Cultural Resources Specialist

THE MATANUSKA COLONY BARNS

Alaska State Library - Historical Collections

THE MATANUSKA COLONY BARNS

The Matanuska Colony Barns

by James H. Fox

Facing page: The Larsh-Wilson barn, tracts no. 31 and 32, later the Linn-Breeden barn, now at the Museum of Alaska Transportation and Industry (photo by Stewart Amgwert). **Left: Leonard Bergan barn, original tract no. 181, on Bodenburg Loop Road** (photo by Albert Marquez/Planet Earth Adventures). **Above: Arnold Carson dairy barn, tract no. 13 on Fairview Loop Road** (photo courtesy of Margaret Heaven).

In 1935 when the U.S. government started designing the Matanuska Valley Colony, the planners intended for the Colonists to be subsistence farmers - no big dairies or large operations. Later in the summer, while the Colonists were living in tent camps and planning their new lives, new contracts between them and the Alaska Rural Rehabilitation Corporation were being printed by *The Anchorage Daily News* print department, where owner and editor Bob Atwood noticed that subsistence was still the goal of the Project. Three or four years later, as the vacant tracts of departing Colonists went to those who stayed, profitable farming became the motive and goal of the new Farmers' Co-operative.

It was the subsistence idea which was the basis for the design of the iconic Colony barn. Later complaints about the barns and the tracts being too small for a viable business farm can be traced back to this early yet quickly discarded idea.

Practical or not, the barns were designed by the architects living in the tent city under the direction of David Williams, who based the gambrel roofed, cubic design on advice from local Experiment Station founder and Alaskan agriculturalist M. D. Snodgrass.

In 1936, after the Colonists were properly housed and most community buildings built, the big barns were started. Most of the barns were begun in late July with building proceeding well into November, and some barns not started until then. Work went fast. Building a barn with a skilled crew took about three weeks. In summer, crews sometimes worked well past midnight into the sunny northern nights and new days.

Non-Colonist crews of hired carpenters were used to start or even finish a great number of the barns. At a minimum this crew laid out the pilings and joists to start the barns level and square, leaving groups of neighboring Colonists to raise their own barns, as farmers have traditionally done. Over half the barns were built by these gangs of Colonist neighbors - with occasional help from the

THE MATANUSKA COLONY BARNS

"... walls were painted with a white or silver paint ..."

An unidentified man painting the interior of a Colony barn to prepare it for Grade A dairy operation - note the concrete floor, the drainage trough in the floor, and metal stanchions for securing the milk cows during milking. (photo courtesy of Jim Fox)

carpenters. The ARRC saw this as a way to keep the men busy when little else but land clearing work was available. For the men it was one of the few ways they could socialize and size up the worth and talents - or lack of same - of each other, a pattern that would continue through years of planting, harvest, war, and other changes.

Ground floor joists were covered with wide, rough, thick planking for flooring. Beneath this floor was a gap of a foot or so between the bottom joists and the soil, for ventilation and to keep the floor boards from contact with the soil and thereby rotting. In winter the opening around the base of the barns was banked with boards, hay and soil, as were the houses in the first few years. This kept the cold from getting under the barns, and kept the heat in, so the freezing of dripping water and urine could not damage the structures.

Spruce logs for the walls were pre-cut to size and sawn flat on three sides at corporation sawmills. They were quickly stacked, with oakum placed between each course, and holes were drilled through several logs to drive pins down through several courses, especially along the edges where the windows would be. This was to keep the green logs in line as they dried and cured, and to give the walls more solidity. Massive nails nearly a foot long penetrated every two logs to knit it all together.

Once the logs were up, ceiling joists - which became the upper haymow floor joists - were put in, and interior walls framed in, as were the windows and doors. Then flooring for the haymow, usually second grade shiplap lumber, was laid on the diagonal over the joists. Pony walls were framed in around the edge of the haymow floor, and then the roof rafters were raised up from the pony walls and tied together so the men could begin to lay cheaper grade shiplap horizontally across the rafters to create the gambrel roof. Slightly better quality shiplap was used on the gable end walls, as well as the upright 3' boards for the pony walls.

The massive haymow door opening was framed in on the front gable end and a door built to seal it, hinged on the bottom so the door closed by being pulled up. Many barns had a pulley system along the main

THE MATANUSKA COLONY BARNS

"...barns began to be seen as picturesque liabilities..."

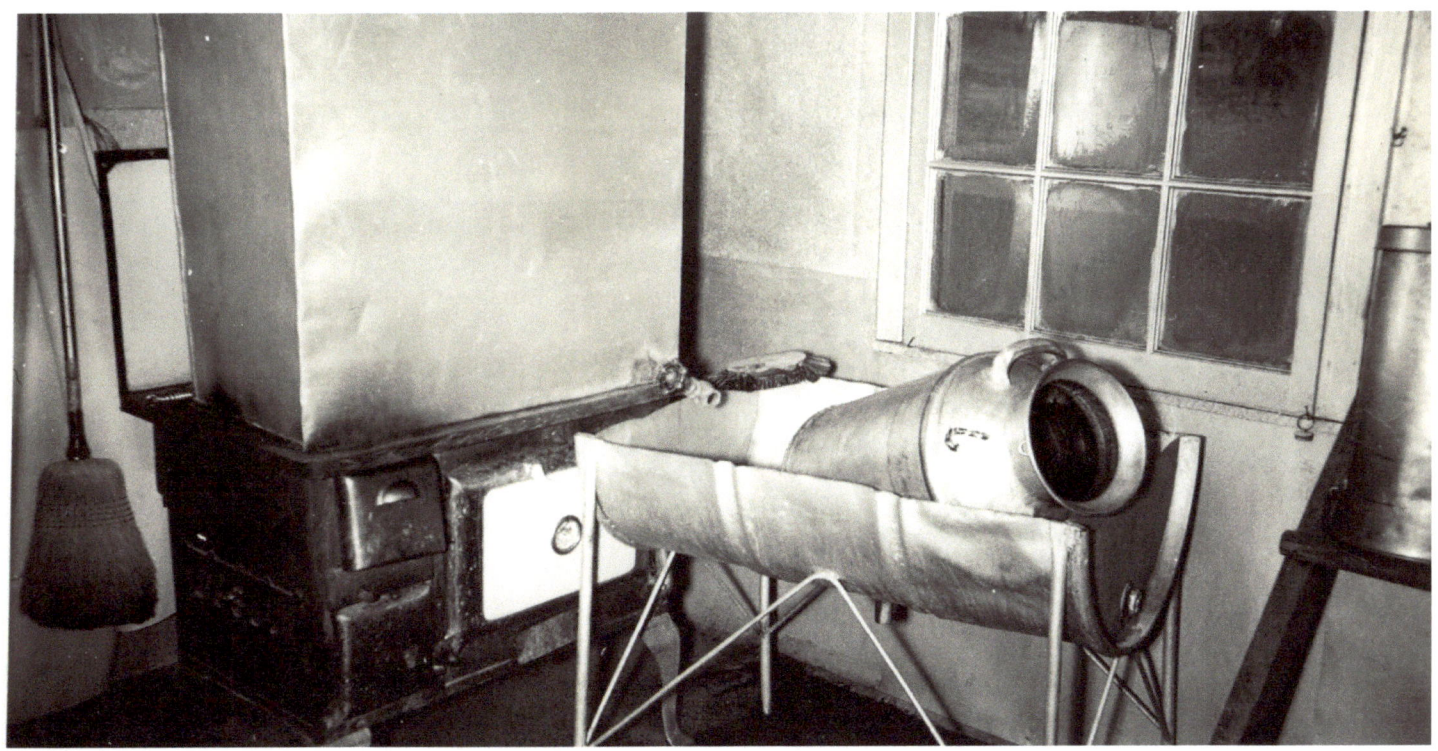

A Colony pump house which has been converted into a milk house. Note the wood cookstove with a large water tank for boiling water to sterilize the milk cans in the sink, which is made from one half of a 50 gallon drum. (photo courtesy of Jim Fox)

roof beam rigged with a giant claw to be let down outside the barn to grab loose hay, then pulled it in through the haymow door. Two smaller doors that fit into the pony walls were made at either end, or in the case of Walter Pippels' side-door barn, above the side entry and exit doors.

A cupola vent was built in the roof center - often with a star or diamond shaped vent cut into the back wall near the gable. Vents from the ground floor went through the roof at the back corners. Rolled roofing ran horizontally or vertically on the roof, held down with roofing nails and lath strips parallel to the seams. Windows, doors, interior wall siding, and a ladder or stairway to the haymow completed the barn. The frame walls were painted red, a rust-red or white. Some farmers peeled the bark off the logs, varnishing or oiling them. Window frames were painted red or white or green. Interior walls and doors were also painted.

By the late 1940s Grade A dairies were the future. This required many changes to the barns: concrete foundations and floors, sometimes only in half of the barn, with troughs along the stalls to wash out the manure and muck. Wooden stations were replaced by metal ones. Milk houses or parlors were attached to the barns. They had concrete floors, too, and were often made from the pump houses from abandoned tracts. Walls were painted with a white or silver paint considered "sanitary" and easier to clean. A large concrete or metal basin was made with two deep sinks - one for cooling the milk in clean milk cans and one for washing and cleaning the cans and milking machines. A wood stove heated the water. An electric pump ran the milking machines.

Agriculture is a turbulent business, dependent on weather, whims, and markets, as well as the age and energy of the farmer. Thirty years after they arrived, some Colonists begin to look at retiring. The market wasn't growing. Children weren't interested in farming. Cattle were sold off. Some barns remained in use, others were simply maintained for storage. Others had no investments made in their upkeep. As owners' interests flagged, the latter barns began to be seen as picturesque liabilities, and many were torn down or allowed to sag into distorted shapes of their former selves. ~•~

THE MATANUSKA COLONY BARNS

"Those who seek the spirit of America might do well to look first in the countryside, for it was there that the spirit was born."
　　　　　　　　　　　　　　　Eric Sloane, **An Age of Barns**

The Legacy of the Colony Barns

Facing page: Venne barn, on the Wes Grover farm (photo by Albert Marquez). Left: Joe Lentz barn (photo by Stewart Amgwert). Above: Detail of Venne barn (Eric Vercammen/Northern Light Media)

A Vital Image

At the *Old House Journal* website, Michael J. Auer wrote, "From the days when Thomas Jefferson envisioned the new republic as a nation dependent on citizen farmers for its stability and its freedom, the family farm has been a vital image in the American consciousness."

Old barns are popular subjects for painters, photographers, and others with an intrinsic appreciation for form, shape, line, color, and history. When one steps inside an old barn, the complex network of beams, braces, posts, rafters and other elements of the barn's framework make an imposing and impressive sight. The rhythmic placement of the structural members creates patterns, and when a dusty light filters through the cracks, an old barn can evoke the same respectful, reverent feelings as one finds when entering an ancient cathedral.

The special character of barns stems from their overall appearance of strength, solidity and permanence. They were built to serve generations of farm families, and over many years of service to those families they would develop a rich patina and a nostalgic appeal to the sensibilities.

Barns are... Sublime

In an article for the National Barn Alliance's publication, *The Barn Journal*, Charles Bultman, an architect in Michigan who has been saving and adapting old barns for many uses, wrote, "Barns in our landscape are sublime. Like a mountain or a river, they have existed there for so long that you can come to believe they will be there forever. But they will not."

In another article for the *Barn Journal*, Catherine A. Brau, a Historic Preservation student at the University of Mary Washington, wrote, "Historic barns – and farmsteads in general – are truly becoming a thing of the past as a result of commercialization and evolving technology and the poor maintenance of outdated or unnecessary structures."

The impermanence of barns can be easily seen in the number of Colony barns which have disappeared in various ways over the decades, whether lost to wind or fire, or disassembled or destroyed when they were no longer needed. Fewer than half of the original structures remain, and many of those are in irreparable condition. The Colony barns are part of Alaska's history and heritage; we should do what we can to save them.

THE MATANUSKA COLONY BARNS

"... a compact square barn..."

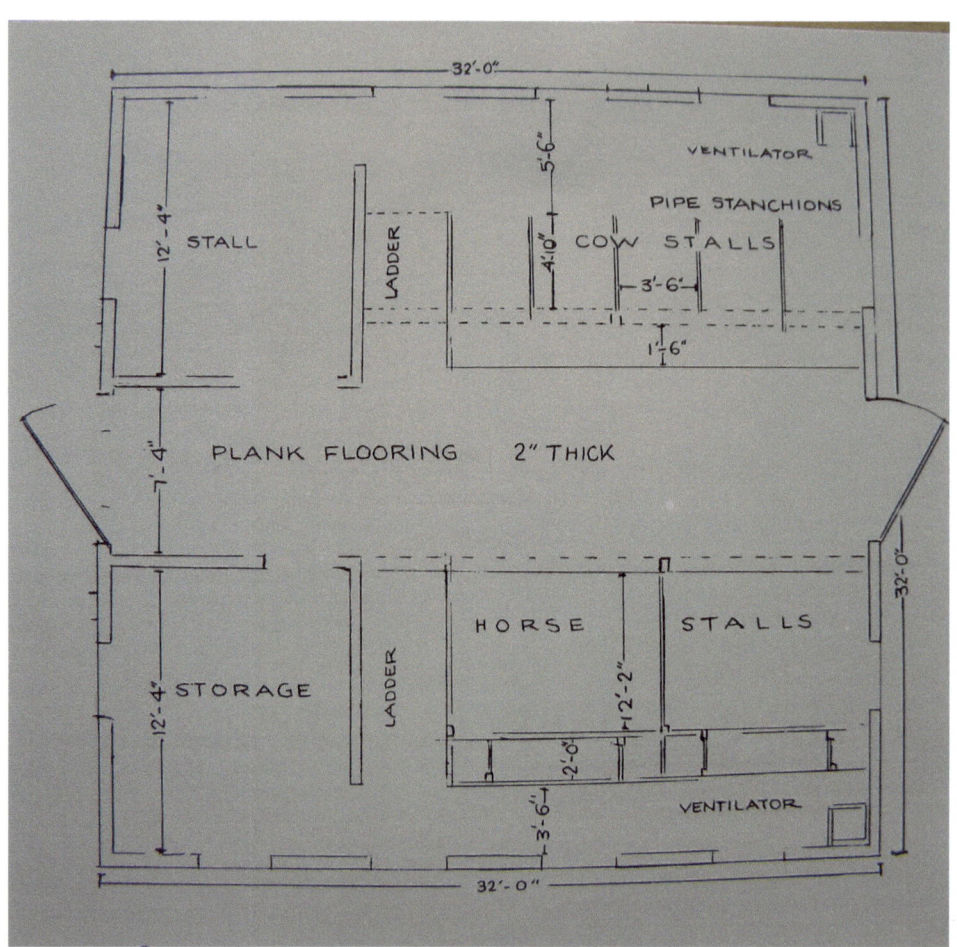

Facing page: Detail of blueprints of the standard Colony barn with gambrel roof **Left:** Barn blueprints interior detail (both FERA Matanuska Colony Architectural Drawings). **Above:** Barn under construction (University of Alaska Fairbanks photograph UAF19680000400964)

A Barn 32' x 32' x 32'

The standard barn built for the Matanuska Colony farmers was a 32' x 32' structure with a gambrel roof soaring another 32' into the air. In a booklet published by the Matanuska-Susitna Borough Division of Cultural Resources in 1988, titled *Evaluation of Historic Sites in Palmer, Alaska*, a description of the barns is given: "The roof ridge projects over the haymow track and has a flared, open eave line. An open cupola provides venting through the center of the ridge. One and one-half stories in height, the lower floor is log and the upper floor is frame. The mid-section or 'pony wall' was usually made of board and batten or vertical planks while drop siding sheathed the hay loft. A large square door, either hinged or on sliding track, provided entry to the hay loft while large, double-leaf doors provided ground floor entrance. Fixed glass, multi-pane windows were used on both floors."

The end result was a compact square barn which was pleasing to look at, but not always pleasing to the farmers who were destined to utilize the barns in their daily lives.

Construction of the Barns Lagged

In *Matanuska Valley Memoir: The Story of How One Alaskan Community Developed*, by Hugh A. Johnson and Keith L. Stanton, published in 1955 by the University of Alaska's Agricultural Experiment Station in Palmer, the authors explained the discontent this one design engendered amongst the farmers: "Construction of the barns lagged. Only one plan was available. Each was 32 feet square, 32 feet high and had a 'hip' roof. The walls were logs to 10 feet above the ground and then siding to the roof. All were built on small pilings of native spruce which soon rotted away. The Colonists complained from the start that the barns were too small, inefficiently partitioned, drafty and poorly built.

THE MATANUSKA COLONY BARNS

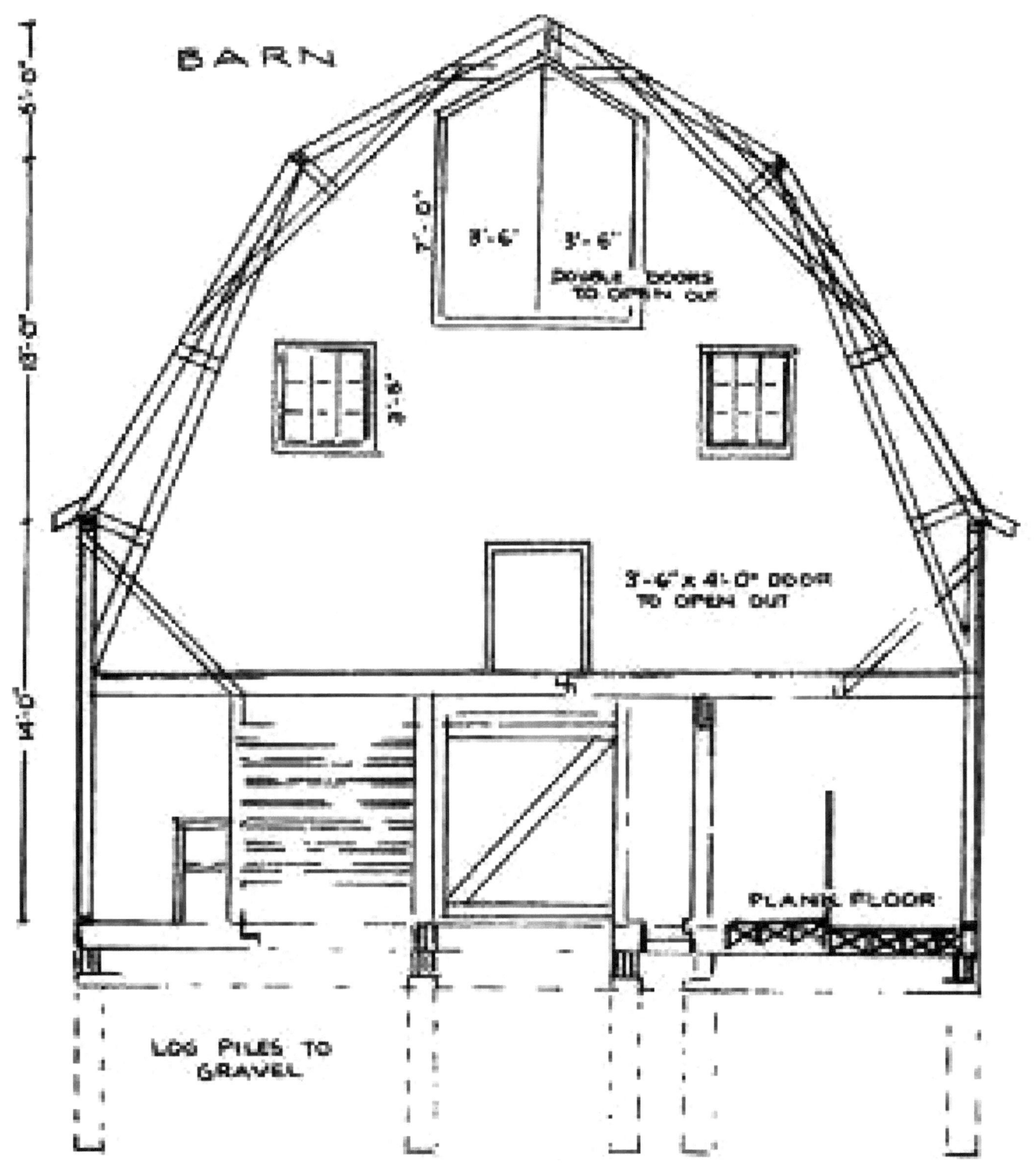

THE MATANUSKA COLONY BARNS

STOREROOM REQUISITION
ALASKA RURAL REHABILITATION CORPORATION

Reg. No. ....
(For use of Property Clerk)

To: PROPERTY CLERK
Please furnish bearer with the following, to be used for **BARN**

Work Order No. **B-2**

JR-54

Quantity	Description	Classification	Price	Amount	✓
7	COLLAR-BEAMS	35	40.00	1 40	
50	SCABS - 2x6	75	40.00	3 00	
50	SCABS - 1x6 50 only	38	30.00	1 14	
2500	B.F. SHIPLAP	2500	36.00	90 00	
52	OVERHANG RAFTERS	156	40.00	6 24	
500	L.F. 1x6 - S-4-S	250	36.00	9 00	
80	L.F. 2x8 - S-4-S	107	37.00	3 96	
25	2x4 - 18' S-4-S	300	37.00	11 10	
25	2x6 - 18' S-4-S	450	40.00	18 00	
1000	L.F. 2x6 ROUGH	1000	30.00	30 00	
400	L.F. 1x2	400	.03	12 00	
300	L.F. 1x4	100	55.00	5 50	
22	HINGES 8"	22	.47	10 34	
12	" 6"	12	.29	3 48	
2	HASP 6"	2	.37½	75	
2	GR-SCREWS	2	.52	1 04	
10	BOLTS ½ x 6"	10	.05	50	
14	BARN-SASH	14	2.06	28 84	
6	INTAKE-VENTS	6	1.50	9 00	
1	CUPELO	1	15.50	15 50	
20	pcs - 2x4 - 16' ROUGH	213	30.00	6 39	
1	pc. 2x12 - 18' S-4-S	36	36.00	1 30	
1	pc. 2x12 - 20' S-4-S	40	36.00	1 44	
1	SET - DOORS				
4	pcs - 2x12 - 16' S-4-S	128	36.00	4 61	
6	2x6 - 18' S-4-S	108	40.00	4 32	
500	B.F. SHIPLAP	500	36.00	18 00	
20	ROLLS ROOFING	20	3.84	76 80	
50	LBS - " NAILS	½	12.85	6 43	

Delivered to | Date delivered | Entered on stock records | Signed | 380.08

THE MATANUSKA COLONY BARNS

"The criticisms were apparently justified..."

The three photos on these pages comprise part of a requisitioning of materials for construction of a Colony barn on tract number 54, for George Campbell. Note the cost of labor included in the final tally of $1,596.36. (Photos by Joanie Juster from original Matanuska Colony Project papers at the National Archives in Anchorage, Alaska)

The criticisms were apparently justified. Dairymen going into Grade A production had to spend large sums to make their barns useable. Some families sold their outbuildings. Many others have abandoned their barns and have allowed them to rot away -- a complete loss and temporary monuments to regimentation.

"The entire building program was poorly planned and poorly executed. Costs mounted to over double the original estimates. Inefficiency, waste, and discouragement were common and served to discourage many families. By July, 1936 67 families of the original Colonists had been sent back to the States soured on Alaska and on the Project."

But even as many families were leaving the Colony, many others were finding plenty to appreciate about their new home and were busily making plans to upgrade and improve their farms. And to be fair, the authors of *Matanuska Valley Memoir* included an explanation breaking down the statistics and determined that "...no less than a fourth of the original Colonists were unsuited physically or mentally for colonization."

Self-Sufficient General Farmers

The families who stayed to build farms on their Colony tracts were a hardy pioneer bunch, but even so, the road to successful farming in Alaska was rough and littered with sizable potholes. Assessing the situation in 1955, the authors of *Matanuska Valley Memoir* noted, "In view of the Colonization history.... it is significant that few people of the Valley were full-time farmers after nearly 15 years of effort -- even though the area included the largest area of cropped and cleared land in Alaska."

The authors contend that the original planners of the Matanuska Colony did not intend for the families to become commercial farmers, or to run specialized farming operations,

59

THE MATANUSKA COLONY BARNS

"The barns are an intrinsic part of the legacy..."

Left: Walter Pippel barn under construction. (Mary Nan Gamble Collection ASL-P270-317 Alaska State Library) **Above: Water tower built winter 1935/36.** (Helen Hegener/Northern Light Media). **Facing page: Appraisal, June 9, 1936.** (photo by Joanie Juster from the 'Campbell, Geo.' file, ARRC papers at the National Archives in Anchorage, Alaska).

but rather to become self-sufficient general farmers. Still, by 1940 there were 83 general farms, 9 dairy farms, 6 truck farms, 2 poultry farms, 1 sheep farm, and 17 unclassified farms. From the 9 dairies in 1940 the dairy industry in the Valley developed and grew until there were 38 Grade A dairies in 1938.

Legacy of the Matanuska Barns

The remaining Matanuska Colony barns can be found in all stages of repair and disrepair, from beautifully restored barns which will enchant many generations yet to come, to collapsing and decaying remnants of the originals, slowly being reclaimed by the land. There is no unified effort to save the remaining barns, although three farms have been added to the National Register of Historic Places, which is the nation's official list of cultural resources worthy of preservation: the Bailey, Patten, and Rebarchek Colony farms. These three barns are included in this book.

There have been singular efforts to save other Colony barns, most notably the Wineck barn at the Alaska State Fairgrounds, the Linn-Breeden barn at the Museum of Alaska Transportation and Industry, and the Stahler and Jensen barns which were rescued and rebuilt to house a doctor's office and other businesses by Doug Olson, who has saved many local barns from an untimely demise. Many individuals have likewise rescued and restored barns, whether their own family's barn or that of a friend or neighbor. At least one barn has been saved because it lends a picturesque ambiance to a neighborhood, which perhaps is as good a reason to save one of these icons as any other.

The history of the Matanuska Colony is an important part of the history of Alaska, and the barns are an intrinsic part of the legacy. Only a handful of their numbers remain, and sadly, too many of those are already beyond salvaging. ~•~

We, the undersigned, having been notified that we were appointed to estimate and appraise the real property on Tract No. 54 held by Geo. Campbell have attended to the duties assigned us, and after a strict examination and careful inquiry, we do estimate and appraise the same as follows:

				Total
Land:	2	Acres Cleared @		
		Acres partially cleared @	$ 50 00	$ 100 00
	38	Acres uncleared @	7 50	285 00
LAND TOTAL				385 00
		Material	Labor	
House: Log, Type ___ or				
X Frame, " 4		1450 00	680 00	2130 00
Barn:		210 00	90 00	300 00
Outside toilet:		16 00	9 00	25 00
Chicken House:				
Well House:				
BUILDINGS: TOTAL				$2455 00
Well:				
Fencing: 86				602 00
TOTAL APPRAISED VALUE				$3442 00

Board of Appraisal

Date June 9, 1936

THE MATANUSKA COLONY BARNS

JOSEPH LENTZ BARN (LEFT), GLENDON DOUGHTY BARN (RIGHT), BOTH BY ALBERT MARQUEZ

THE MATANUSKA COLONY BARNS

PART TWO - THE BARNS

THE MATANUSKA COLONY BARNS

Bailey / Estelle

Photo above: East side of the Bailey-Estelle barn (Eric Vercammen/Northern Light Media) **Photo at left: Ferber Bailey farm circa 1955 (**Library of Congress, Prints & Photographs Division HABS AK, 13-PALM.V,4-1) **Facing page: The Bailey-Estelle barn and Pioneer Peak, Fall, 2008** (Helen Hegener/Northern Light Media)

Bailey / Estelle
3150 North Glenn Highway, Marsh Road

Ferber and Ruth Bailey of Lena, Wisconsin, joined the Colony trek in 1935 with their two children. Ferber, who drew tract no. 152, was a carpenter by trade, and he dug a full basement and then helped build their unique home, a one-and-one-half story frame building. The house has a gambrel roof matching the barn, a departure from the norm which makes the entire farm scene unusual and visually appealing, particularly when viewed with 6,398' Pioneer Peak soaring in the background.

The barn built for Ferber Bailey in 1936 is described in detail on the National Register of Historic Places registration form: "The barn, measuring 32' x 32', is a typical gambrel-roofed Colony barn with flared eaves. It is of log and frame construction. Small, one-story wood-sided shed additions have been attached on the north and south facades. The original barn is intact and its front facade is unchanged. The barn sits on a concrete sill added when the building was moved. The first floor logs are covered with horizontal lap siding--it is the only colony barn originally constructed with siding over the logs. The upper floor, under the roof line, is sheathed with horizontal drop siding. The mid-section is covered with vertical boards. An open cupola, which vents the building, is located in the center of the high roof ridge. The roof eave extends over the hay loft door on the west side. The door is flanked by multi-pane windows, identical to those on the first floor. The first floor has standard double and single doors.

"The barn stands approximately 150 feet from its original site. It was moved in the late 1940s when the adjacent Glenn Highway was widened." ~•~

THE MATANUSKA COLONY BARNS

"The farm sits at the top of Bailey Hill, north of Palmer..."

Left: East side. Above: West side. Below left: Looking north. Below right: North side shed, stored lumber. Facing page: West side. (All photos on these two pages by Eric Vercammen/Northern Light Media)

THE MATANUSKA COLONY BARNS

THE MATANUSKA COLONY BARNS

Wilson / Larsh / Linn / Breeden / MATI

Facing page: Interior of hayloft showing the old timbers (photo by Ron Day/RonDayView Photography) **Above: The barn after the restoration work has begun at the Museum of Alaska Transportation and Industry in Wasilla.** (photo by Stewart Amgwert)

Wilson/Larsh/Linn/Breeden/MATI
Museum of Alaska Transportation and Industry, 3800 W. Museum Dr, Wasilla

The large double barn at the Museum of Alaska Transportation and Industry (MATI) is known locally as the Linn-Breeden barn, created from two separate Colony barns by an early valley homesteader named Frank Linn, whose son Allan grew up to be the State Director of Agriculture from 1975 to 1979.

Frank Linn came to Alaska in 1927 and spent three years working at the Matanuska Experiment Station. In 1928 he purchased 160 prime acres on the southern border of the Station, on a bluff with a commanding view of Pioneer Peak and the Chugach Mountains. In 1935 he sold his land to the Alaska Rural Rehabilitation Corporation (ARRC) for $5.09 an acre. Colonist Amedee Wilson won the choice tract in the original drawing, but in 1937 Amedee, his wife Leah, and their four children left Alaska.

Frank and Vera Linn acquired the tract again in 1938, and in 1941 they added the neighboring tract, which had been won by Emil Larsh. The Linn family developed a dairy farm, and in 1943 they moved the Larsh barn adjacent to the Wilson barn at a right angle, creating the immense 85-foot-long by 28-foot-wide structure.

In 1957, Anchorage dairy farmers Don and LaVera Breeden purchased the Linn dairy and in 1958 they moved their operation to the Matanuska Valley. The dairy farm eventually changed into a vegetable farm, then became the Matanuska Riding Stables and Guest Ranch, and in later years the Matanuska Lake RV Park.

Upon retiring the Breeden family donated the barn to the Museum of Alaska Transportation and Industry, and in the early morning hours of August 26, 2007, the giant structure was carefully moved to its new home.

THE MATANUSKA COLONY BARNS

"The nine mile trip took five hours..."

Above: In the early morning hours of July 17, 2007 the immense Linn-Breeden barn was trucked through downtown Wasilla to its new location at the Museum of Alaska Transportation and Industry (Frontiersman staff photo by Robert DeBerry, Mat-Su Valley Frontiersman). **Right:** Kelley Griffin and Ralph Breeden at the Breeden farm, circa 1970 (photo courtesy of Kelley Griffin).

In a July, 2007 article for *The Mat-Su Valley Frontiersman*, JJ Harrier wrote an article about how funds were raised for the epic undertaking, explaining that the Museum of Alaska Transportation and Industry (MATI) sponsored an old-fashioned "hoe-down" event which drew donations toward the costs of moving and stabilizing the huge structure on its new foundation.

Harrier wrote, "As the afternoon progressed... patrons ate barbecue favorites, stared up at the massive red barn and asked each other how mankind could possibly move something so immense."

A request from the Executive Director of MATI for assistance with the traffic signals noted that six intersections with signals would be crossed en route along the Parks Highway. From the letter:

"Hermon Rd. signal is on cables. However, there is a frontage road we will use to go around the signal. Hence, no conflicts.

"The Palmer-Wasilla signal is on arms and the arms are at a distance apart allowing us to maneuver around them without any conflict.

"Crusey St. could possibly be also maneuvered through. However it could possibly take more time and delays than were one of the arms swung out of the way. Main Street and Lucas Roads must have one of the arms moved.

"Church Rd. is a major problem. This light is on cables. The lights are too low to lift and there is no possible means of going around."

The Executive Director's request to three local electric companies to assist with the predicament ended with, "Exactly how this would be accomplished I need to leave up to your companies for input."

The nine-mile trip took five hours to complete. The barn is currently undergoing restoration at MATI. ~•~

THE MATANUSKA COLONY BARNS

71

Joseph Puhl farm, circa 1955. (Library of Congress Prints & Photographs Division HABS AK 13-PALM.V, 5-1)

Puhl / Wilson / Miller / Bacon

Puhl / Wilson / Miller / Bacon home and barn from the Glenn Highway, north of Palmer. (Helen Hegener/Northern Light Media)

Puhl / Wilson / Miller / Bacon
13151 E. Scott Road

Joseph and Blanche Puhl and their two sons, Lloyd and Raymond, came to Palmer from Rice Lake, Wisconsin, and they were one of the first three Colonist families to go off relief, which was played up by the Alaska Rural Rehabilitation Corporation and F.D.R.'s administration (the other families were those of Colonists Virgil Eckert and Walter Pippel).

The Puhl's unique round-log house is on the National Register of Historic Places. Unlike most of the Colony houses, it was built by the owners, with the assistance of other Colonists, during the summer of 1936. The Puhls dug their own well instead of waiting for the corporation well rig, which also helped to limit the Puhls' indebtedness to the ARRC.

Located on Tract 99 at what is now the corner of the Glenn Highway and Scott Road, the Puhl barn is also a departure from the standard Colony barn design by government architect David R. Williams. Like their neighbors and good friends the Eckerts, who selected tract no. 100, the Puhls built a smaller, barrel vault-roofed barn (28' x 32'), as compared to the standard 32' x 32' gambrel-roofed Colony barn.

THE MATANUSKA COLONY BARNS

"In 1958 Dexter Bacon moved the barn..."

Left: rear of the barn. Above: A quilt hangs in the upper window. Facing page: The barrel vault roofed Puhl barn is one of four with this unusual design, the others were owned by Colonists Eckert, Arndt, and Monroe. (All photos by Helen Hegener/ Northern Light Media)

Moved in 1958

According to the book, *Evaluation of Historic Sites in Palmer, Alaska*, printed in September, 1988 by the Matanuska-Susitna Borough Cultural Resources Division, "The barn originally stood on the northern end of the Puhl tract and had a first floor of log. Because it was built without a foundation, as was typical, the logs began deteriorating.

"In 1958 Dexter Bacon moved the barn to its present location and substituted a short concrete block wall and concrete slab floor. The laminated ribs now rest directly on the concrete block. The domed roof flares at the bottom. The barn is sided with drop siding and has fixed, six-pane windows. Large doors are located on either end. The building is currently used as a garage."

A barrel vault, also known as a tunnel vault or a wagon vault, is an architectural element formed by the extrusion of a single curve - or pair of curves, in the case of this barn's pointed barrel vault roof - with the length being greater than its diameter.

The history of the property is also described in the Mat-Su Borough book: "In October 1942 the Puhls sold their land to Carl Wilson, who took over the Puhl's obligation to the ARRC. In 1954 the Wilsons sold the land to Neil Miller, who later sold it to his daughter and son-in-law, Dexter and Priscilla Miller Bacon."

As noted in the National Register of Historic Places listing, the house and property exhibit attention to detail and excellent care. An interesting side note is a newspaper report in the *Milwaukee Journal* dated May 15, 1935, describing young Raymond Puhl, age 7, having contracted a mild case of measles and being completely segregated from the other passengers due to the contagious nature of the disease. However: "His sickness will not prevent his sailing Saturday..." ~•~

THE MATANUSKA COLONY BARNS

Loyer / Lake

Opposite page: Loyer barn, with portions of the Lake barn addition visible as the low-roofed gray structure. Above photos: hexagonal silo and detail. (all: Helen Hegener/Northern Light Media)

Loyer / Lake
Outer Springer Loop Road

On a blustery fall day sisters Rita and Dottie Loyer shared the history of their unique and lovingly restored family barn, which was rebuilt as a wider, lower structure than the original Colony barn, combining elements of Colonist John Lake's barn from tract #73, just up the road at the corner of Inner and Outer Springer Loop Roads.

Rita said that her older brother James remembered their father purchasing the Lake barn from the ARRC, perhaps after the Lake family went back to Wisconsin.

The Loyer barn, on tract no. 62, was originally about 150 feet closer to the house, which had been built in the summer of 1935. Reconstruction of the Loyer barn took place beginning in 1946 with moving the barn to its present location, and Rita Loyer thought the first silo was also built around that time.

The silo is a beautiful hexagonal structure of 2" x 4"s laid flat, on a hexagonal concrete foundation. The second silo, which Rita Loyer thought had been built later than the first, was blown over in a windstorm many years ago. There are plans to replace it eventually. Rita Loyer shared a specially commissioned art print by local artist Shane Lamb, showing the Loyer farm as it looked in its original layout, with the barn to the south of the house and the well pumphouse close to the east side of the house. Pioneer Peak looms in the background, and in real life the great peak is indeed there, just a few miles south of the family's home.

The Loyer barn stores life-size farm animals and elements of farm life which are utilized in Palmer displays and parades, for which the Loyers have won many accolades and awards. Their ongoing project to restore the barn of their childhood continues, with their focus turning to the interior repairs now. ~•~

THE MATANUSKA COLONY BARNS

"A lovingly restored barn..."

Facing page: The Loyer farm, by Palmer artist Shane Lamb. Above and left; the silo. Below left: the front of the reconstructed barn, and a snowmachine whimsically placed on the roof. Below right: the back side of the barn showing part of the Lake barn addiition (gray with white trim), and the base of the collapsed second silo. (All photos: Helen Hegener/Northern Light Media)

THE MATANUSKA COLONY BARNS

79

THE MATANUSKA COLONY BARNS

Havemeister

The picturesque Havemeister Dairy barn, near the intersection of Bogard and Trunk Roads, has been expanded and added onto over the years to keep up with the demands of the successful dairy operation, but the unmistakeable origins can be seen in the Colony barn's distinctive lines. (All photos by Helen Hegener/Northern Light Media)

Havemeister
Bogard Road, Palmer

The Havemeister Dairy, still family owned and operated after 77 years, is the only working dairy farm which is still in existence from the original Matanuska Colony. Arnold and Emmy Havemeister joined the Colony from Michigan. They built their home, which is still in the Havemeister family today, on tract number 167, near the present-day intersection of Bogard and Trunk Roads, just a few miles east of Wasilla.

Arnold and Emmy worked hard to develop their dairy, but in September, 1942, only seven years after drawing their 40 acres of land in the lottery, Arnold passed away, leaving Emmy a widow with three small children: Helen, Annie, and Bob.

Emmy continued to work the farm and she and her children built the dairy into what it is today. A 2002 article for *The Mat-Su Frontiersman* quoted the Havemeister's daughter, Helen Riley, talking about her mother, Emmy: ""She loved the Valley. She said there was no place in all of the world like Alaska, and the Valley was the best place in all of Alaska. This was her home."

In 2002 Arnold and Emmy's son Bob and his wife Jeanne, who took over operation of the Havemeister Dairy when Emmy retired from active ownership, were recognized as the 2002 Alaska State Fair Farm Family of the Year.

Today the 200 acre Havemeister Dairy farm maintains a herd of 150 cows, and the modern, high-tech operation tracks each cow in the herd. An on-site creamery processes and bottles the milk, which is pasteurized, homogenized, and hormone free. The milk is sold in many local stores in southcentral Alaska.

The beautiful Havemeister Dairy on Bogard Road is a familiar sight to many, evoking fond memories of the Valley's agricultural past. ~•~

THE MATANUSKA COLONY BARNS

Anderson/Vickaryous/Roach/ Luster/Bradley/Stevenson

The Ravens Roost farm on Hyer Road features this Colony barn beautifully restored by the Stevenson family. Facing page: The Ravens Roost barn in 2000, after restoration. Left: The hayloft. Above: Locally harvested three-sided timbers replaced the original spruce logs which were beyond salvaging. (All photos these pages by Stewart Amgwert)

Anderson/Vickaryous/Roach/ Luster/Bradley/Stevenson
Hyer Road, Wasilla

Maureen Stevenson shared her family's experiences with a Colony barn on their farm, Raven's Roost: "It was called the Anderson farm but I know of four other owners: Bradley, Luster, Cappy Roach and Vickaryous. There were others in there…"

Maureen noted that they purchased the farm in 1997, and wrote, "The farm had been rented for quite some time… the house and barn needed so much it was hard to know where to start, as the walls were rotting and the roof was gone."

They hired a local man, John Vosburgh, who "bought local logs to replace more than half of the walls with, and jacked the barn up about 4 ft to work on cement footers and floors in the entry and well room."

The well was replaced, and Maureen explains: "When we had a big job scheduled, such as pouring cement, we would bake rhubarb pies the day before and then bring in friends and family to help. With a promise of pie when the job was finished, we had a steady supply of volunteers, such as my son Reed, who somehow drew the wheelbarrow with the leaky tire. So his route was over to the cement truck for a load in his wheelbarrow, run fast to the pouring site, back out to the air hose, run fast to the cement truck…"

The logs which needed replacing were changed for new logs, and "the Barn Project was progressing well, and we were ready to roof, so out came the tar buckets, tar paper, a truck load of lumber, the longest ladders, and the repaired directional wind vane. We'd found parts of this large bronze hawk in the shed, and took it to Goodrich's Machine Shop in Palmer, where he reassembled it and made the pieces that were missing. Looked good!" ~•~

Johnson / McCombs / Heaven

Left and above: The top section of the barn with like-painted outbuildings (Eric Vercammen/Northern Light Media) *Right: Rails for driving a tractor into the barn* (Helen Hegener/Northern Light Media)

Johnson / McCombs / Heaven
Davis Road, Wasilla

The land which comprised Matanuska Colony tract number 15 was originally homesteaded by A. J. Swanson in the early 1900's, and was purchased by the Federal Government to be included in the colony lottery. Johan Johnson, from Minnesota, who traveled to Alaska with his wife Irene and their young son Anatol, drew the lot for the farm in 1935.

Twenty years later, in 1955, Bob and Merlie McCombs purchased the farm, and they operated a large dairy with Joe and Myrtle Gislason which became a picturesque local landmark on a hillside curve of Fairview Loop Road.

In the late 1990's the upper section of the Johnson barn was acquired by Leroi and Margaret Heaven and moved to their property on Davis Road, about a mile west of the original location of the barn on Colony tract number 15.

Leroi Heaven, who grew up on Fairview Loop Road, only a couple of miles west of the Johnson farm, said, "There were eleven farms on Fairview Loop when I was growing up, and nine of them were dairies."

Leroi was a lifelong farmer and master organic gardener, and served on the board of the Wasilla-Knik Historical Society and on the borough's Historical Preservation Commission, a government commission established in the 1980s, in part to preserve the architectural heritage of the valley.

Leroi nurtured a longtime interest in saving and restoring historic local buildings, with several of the old structures moved to or rebuilt on his property. In the early 1990's Heaven's farm became the first property in the Matanuska-Susitna Borough to be placed under an agricultural conservation easement, a designation meant to curtail any development other than farming forever. ~•~

THE MATANUSKA COLONY BARNS

THE MATANUSKA COLONY BARNS

"There were eleven farms on Fairview Loop when I was growing up... nine were dairies..." ~Leroi Heaven

Left: Interior showing the roof framing timbers and structure. Above: Front of barn. Right: Leroi Heaven's Ford 9N with snowplow blade attached. Below: An antique haymow pulley. (All photos by Eric Vercammen/Northern Light Media)

THE MATANUSKA COLONY BARNS

Lentz / Musk Ox Farm

The William Lentz barn, now the Musk Ox Farm, on Archie Road, north of Palmer. Above: Looking directly up into the rooftop cupola. Right: Interior endwall of the hayloft, with a unique star-shaped ventilation hole. (Photos by Helen Hegener/Northern Light Media)

Lentz / Musk Ox Farm
12850 E. Archie Rd., Palmer

There were two Lentz families among the Colonists, and they were both from Merrill, Wisconsin, but they did not travel together, nor did they arrive in the Valley together. Joseph Lentz arrived with his wife, Zuelika, and their six children, and he drew tract number 183, on the west side of Bodenburg Butte. Photos of their large white dairy barn can be found elsewhere in this book.

Joseph's brother William arrived with his wife, Viola, and one child, and drew tract no. 133. at the end of what became Archie Road, north of Palmer.

The William Lentz barn is now the museum and gift shop for the Musk Ox Farm, home to a lively herd of sixty musk ox, where the dedicated staff continues a unique domestication project begun by an Arctic researcher and visionary farmer named John Teal.

Founded in 1954, the Musk Ox Project has a clear mission statement: "The Musk Ox Farm is a non-profit organization dedicated to the domestication of the musk ox and to the promotion of qiviut production as a gentle and sustainable agricultural practice in the far north, with a focus on public education and providing additional income opportunities to Alaskan natives."

At the farm, the musk oxen are combed and the qiviut is delivered to the native knitters' cooperative, which then spins the wool and sends the yarn to their members in remote Alaskan villages, who knit hats, scarves, and 'nachaqs' (or Eskimo smoke-rings) in delicate lacy patterns inspired by traditional village designs. The luxurious finished creations are sent back to Anchorage and then sold world-wide, supplementing many of the members' largely subsistence lifestyle with cash income. ~•~

THE MATANUSKA COLONY BARNS

Wineck / Alaska State Fair

Facing page: Wineck barn at the Alaska State Fairgrounds. (Eric Vercammen/ Northern Light Media). **This barn also appears on the cover. Above: Wineck barn around 1980, after being moved from the Butte area.** (Library of Congress Photos & Prints Division HABS AK 13-PALM, V, 3A-1) **Left: Window and vent** (Helen Hegener/Northern Light Media).

Wineck / Alaska State Fair
Alaska State Fairgrounds, Palmer

Pioneer Ed Wineck, son of the Klondike goldrush miner Uldrick Wineck, first travelled to Alaska in 1919. After several years he returned to Michigan, heading north again with his brother in 1934 and eventually finding work supplying timbers for the Jonesville mines north of Palmer. In 1936, after some of the original Colonists returned to the states, Ed Wineck became a replacement Colonist, and drew tract no. 174, which was situated on the western side of Bodenburg Butte. Being an experienced carpenter, he supervised the construction of barns for neighboring families, as well as working on the community center, school, and the ARRC building.

At the 2012 Alaska State Fair Ed's son Earl explained some of the details of the barn to the author, starting with the ventilation system: "The cows, in the winter even, kept that place at seventy degrees all the time. At one time we had about four cows and a couple of horses, and sheep and we even had some pigs in there. They put out a lot of heat!"

The Winecks farmed for over 40 years, starting the Valley's first poultry farm in 1937, and supplying milk to the co-op. Asked if he helped his father with building the barn Earl, who was eight years old at the time, replied "Oh, I pounded a few nails…"

He continued, "They had a sawmill in the area and they'd bring the logs down to the sawmill and cut them up, into whatever people wanted, like the three-sided ones that they used for the lower part. For the joists and siding, they were rough lumber. Now if you went upstairs and looked, that's dimensional lumber. Rough lumber is about two inches, but dimensional lumber is if you wanted two inches you got two inches, or an

THE MATANUSKA COLONY BARNS

"...it was too wide to pass through the bridges..."

Left: New lumber down the center of the interior marks where the two halves of the barn were spliced back together after moving. Above: Bracing supports were added to stabilize the structure for transport. Facing page: The lower ten feet of each barn was built with logs from the immediate area, milled at the sawmills set up at each camp. (Helen Hegener/Northern Light Media)

inch and a quarter, or whatever, it had to be dimensional to be able to build that framework to hold up the roof... It was a special design that my father knew, and that's where they really needed his help. Putting the logs up, those guys could do that, but that big roof was far more technical."

"They used green lumber, and they had to compensate for the shrinkage when they dried out, so they had big long iron bars that they ran down through holes drilled in the walls so the logs would settle. They couldn't nail them together or they'd be gapping all over. I don't know if my dad figured that out, but he knew about the shrinkage, and then if the logs appeared to be checking, they put spikes in them to stop it."

In 1973 Earl talked his father, Ed Wineck, into donating the barn to the Alaska State Fair, but the barn was too wide to pass through either of the narrow steel bridges across the Knik and Matanuska Rivers. It was not until the new Knik River Bridge was built in 1976 that the barn could actually be transported to the state fairgrounds near Palmer. The elder Wineck oversaw the job of breaking the barn into pieces suitable for transporting.

The great structure was heavily braced for travel stresses, then sawn in half from the front door to the rear door. It was loaded onto flatbed trailers and moved down Bodenburg Loop Road, then south on the Old Glenn Highway, past the Eklutna Power Station. The trucks turned north onto the Parks Highway, crossed the Knik River and then across the Palmer Hay Flats and back up the new Glenn Highway to the Fairgrounds. There the two halves were expertly aligned and spliced together again.

On August 28, 1977 the Alaska State Fair celebrated Ed Wineck Day, and on September 14, 1977 the barn was officially gifted to the Alaska State Fair. Today the magnificent barn is a favorite with fair visitors, and it stands as an enduring tribute to the pioneer spirit. ~•~

THE MATANUSKA COLONY BARNS

THE MATANUSKA COLONY BARNS

THE MATANUSKA COLONY BARNS

"...the two halves were expertly spliced together..."

Facing page: Side windows small square screened windows for cross-ventilation. Lower left: Plaque above the front door. (both by Eric Vercammen/ Northern Light Media). Left: Bracing inside the hayloft. Above: Lap-sided boards form the ventilation shafts inside Lower right: The roof structure of the Wineck barn. (photos by Helen Hegener/ Northern Light Media).

Parks / Archer

The Parks/Archer barn is a familiar landmark in the Bodenburg Loop Road area, being two Colony barns placed end-to-end. In the photo on the facing page the barn on the left is the Parks barn, built on tract no. 189, and the barn on the right is the Archer barn, moved from tract no. 193. (Photos by Helen Hegener/Northern Light Media)

Parks / Archer
Bodenburg Loop Road, Palmer

The Parks and Archer barns were built on adjoining 80 acre tracts, numbers 189 and 193, respectively. Lynn Sandvik explained to the author, "They moved the Archer barn north and put them together and did quite a bit of work on them about 20 years ago, for some kind of centennial something, but then they forgot about them again."

In a letter to the author, Valley historian Jim Fox related a little of the Parks family history from an interview with daughter Bonita Parks Strong: "Many of the farmers in the Butte had sheep, selling their wool to Pendleton in Washington or Minnesota woolen mills, often getting blankets and winter clothes in exchange along with some cash. The Parks family had a big flock which they drove up into the mountains to the north in the summer, an 18 to 20 mile trip..."

Glen Archer, a grandson of Colonists Perle and Dorothy Archer, wrote to the author, "My sister and I grew up listening to our father, Floyd Archer, tell stories about growing up in the Matanuska Valley and homesteading there and how his parents, Perle and Dorothy Archer, moved the family from Wisconsin to Alaska. He was only 18 months old... there were six children including my father in the family. My father still has lots of memories of life in Alaska, going to school, playing with the Colony kids, and all the hard work and long winters."

"About 12 years ago, I inherited from my father the old family album filled with pictures of the homestead and family in Alaska. Among the pictures is a picture of the Archer barn, more pictures of the chicken coop, farm animals, the fields, as well as the house. All of the pictures appear to have been taken by my great

THE MATANUSKA COLONY BARNS

THE MATANUSKA COLONY BARNS

THE MATANUSKA COLONY BARNS

"Archer barn, it's a dandy... was painted by Vernon Post."

Above top: Postcard showing the Otto Peterson barn and the Archer farm in the distance. Other photographs are from the family album of Perle and Dorothy Archer, taken by Dorothy's mother, Lilian Post, who visited the family in the summer of 1939. Captions are noted in the text below. (Photos on these pages are the property of and used with permission from Glen Archer.)

grandparents (Dorothy's parents) during their trip to visit Perle, Dorothy and the six kids, in 1939, which would have been well after Perle and Dorothy were selected as part of the 200 plus families and moved to Palmer."

In another letter to the author and friends, Glen Archer shared some of the family history after a visit with his father: "Dad said yesterday that the original house was a nice fairly large two story log house which had a full basement. It had been insulated with what he remembers as oakum, which he described as fibers saturated with a tar like substance. Somehow, two or three years after being built, his older siblings Betty and Bob one day caught the insulation on fire and the house burned to the ground. Dad said that grandpa (Perle) was very sad about the whole experience as he had really put his heart and soul into building that place and was proud of it. According to Dad, Grandpa was one of the few individuals who truly knew how to build and taught others to build. He was a general contractor for decades after they returned to the states. Grandpa also apparently started a sawmill which employed others so they could have access to milled lumber and was instrumental in building Fort Richardson."

The photos on these pages show the Archer barn in its original location on tract number 193. The photo on the facing page notes, "Archer barn, it's a dandy, was painted by Vernon Post."

The aerial photo, top center, shows the Peterson barn looking south toward the Archer farm and Pioneer Peak; the photo below it is captioned "This is the way they clear land."

In the photo in front of the Archer barn, the Parks barn can be seen in the distance, along with Bodenburg Butte. Glen Archer's great grandmother Lillian Post wrote near it, "Perle Archer thinks he can handle his big bull..." ~•~

THE MATANUSKA COLONY BARNS

Arndt / Swift

The Arndt/Swift barn on the Palmer-Wasilla Highway was one of only four barrel-vault roofed barns to be built by the Colonists. (Photos by Helen Hegener/Northern Light Media)

Arndt / Swift
10302 E. Palmer-Wasilla Hiway

The Lawrence Arndt family came to Alaska from Wisconsin, and Mr. Arndt drew tract number 190, on what was then called the Wasilla-Finger Lake-Palmer Road, today known as the Palmer-Wasilla Highway. The 1940 census showed Mr. Arndt living with his wife Etta, their 18-year-old daughter Helen; his mother Emma Arndt, and three male lodgers: Edward Church, and Glenn and Rollo Kinty.

The unusual Arndt barn was one of the handful of barns which had a soaring vaulted roof design, with a high ridge peak, quite different from the standard 32' x 32' gambrel roof design of most of the Colonist's barns. Also known as the curved or Gothic roof, the curvature was built up of boards bent to the desired radius and nailed together to provide adequate strength to support the huge roof structure. Like the standard Colony barns, the bottom section was built with three-sided logs, set on spruce pilings. The inside of the barn was partitioned into areas of various sizes, and a storeroom under the steep stairwell which accessed the hayloft.

The Manuska-Susitna Borough's 1985 book, *Knik Matanuska Susitna: A Visual History of the Valleys*, noted: "The Lawrence Arndt colony farm has been familiar to Valley residents for years as Arabian Acres where owners Robert and Gladys Swift raised purebred Morgan horses. The Colony barn was especially designed like the Monroe, Eckert, and Puhl barns, with a high vaulted roof that varied from the standard colony gambrel. During the colony era, the Arndt house was the site of the neighborhood telephone."

Kathy (Roark) Laing, who lived for several years on the adjoining farm with a similar vault roofed barn, wrote that she remembered there being "...three farms in a row..." ~•~

THE MATANUSKA COLONY BARNS

Monroe / Roark

Facing page: Barn with spud cellar below, soon to be wall of milking station, August 1948. Above: Circa 1950. Left: **Original barn with addition of milking station, circa 1950.** (Photos property of Kathy (Roark) Laing, used with permission.)

Monroe / Roark
10539 E. Palmer-Wasilla Hiway

During the editing of this book, Kathy (Roark) Laing, of Blaine, Washington, wrote to the author about her family's Colony barn:

"My family purchased one of the original colonist farms in 1949 from Lester Monroe (Wisconsin). Monroe had had enough of farm life, put the farm up for sale and he and his family moved to Anchorage. We lived there five years. The house is still intact and occupied, I have visited a few times throughout the years. Unfortunately I believe the barn is no longer standing, although I do have pictures of it that were taken while we lived there."

Kathy sent the accompanying photos, which show one of the rare vaulted roofed barns, of which only three others have been documented, those belonging to the Colonists Puhl, Eckert, and Arndt (who drew the Colony tract neighboring Monroe's to the west).

Lester Monroe drew tract number 185, which was the parcel Kathy's family purchased in 1949. Her father, Bill Roark, added a milking station to the barn around 1950, as shown in the photos. Kathy wrote about the long driveway from their house to the road which ran between Palmer and Wasilla, "I remember walking to the school bus every day, it seemed like a mile. It was considerably shortened when the Palmer-Wasilla Road was straightened after we moved."

Kathy continued, "...our barn, on tract number 185, was similar to the red barn on the tract next door *[Editor's note: That would have been the Arndt barn, on tract number 190, see page 101]*. Our barn is no longer there and I vaguely remember someone saying it had been torn down."

Indeed, the Arndt barn is still on the neighboring tract, but the Monroe barn is gone.   ~•~

THE MATANUSKA COLONY BARNS

THE MATANUSKA COLONY BARNS

Rebarchek / Mattson / Keyes

Facing page: Rebarchek farm circa 1955, west side of well house and barn. (Library of Congress, Prints & Photographs Division HABS AK, 13-PALM.V,2-2), **Left: House, wellhouse and barn (**LoC, Photos Div. HABS AK, 13-PALM.V,2-4), **Above: Mattson barn from the Rebarchek farm, now owned by Arthur Keyes.** (Eric Vercammen/Northern Light Media)

Rebarchek / Mattson / Keyes
Inner Springer Loop Rd., Palmer

Along the south side of the Alaska state fairgrounds runs Rebarchek Road, and it was here that Raymond Rebarchek settled his family from Minnesota, on tract number 52.

In his book *Memoirs of an Alaskan Farmer* (Vantage Press, 1980), Raymond Rebarchek described when he first saw the 40 acres he'd drawn in the lottery: "Our place was simply beautiful, gently rolling, with some of the densest timber I ever saw in my life. The heavy growth was probably the result of the rich soil."

In the 1940's the Rebarcheks turned their farm into a fully modern Grade A dairy, with up to 36 milk cows in their parlor. They also farmed potatoes, and at one point had 28 acres of peas. Raymond explains in his book, "You got a cash crop for the peas, silage for the cows, and it built up the soil. I have been partial to peas from the beginning."

In 1969 the Rebarcheks retired from the dairy business. Raymond took up growing prize-winning cabbages for the State Fair as a hobby, with varying amounts of success. Years of experimentation led to friendly competition with another Palmer grower of large cabbages, Max Sherrod, and the two men traded championship cabbage wins for several years.

The original Rebarchek barn burned in 1980, and was replaced with the barn from the Runar Mattson farm, tract no. 43. Today this barn is owned by Arthur Keyes and used as a farm market in the summertime. In 2001 the Alaska State Fair purchased 40 acres of Rebarchek's farmland which had recently been used as a gravel pit, and in 2002, the Fair also purchased the old Rebarchek farmhouse, outbuildings, and five additional acres of land. ~•~

THE MATANUSKA COLONY BARNS

Sjodin / Klem / Sojka

Left and facing page: Sjodin barn, Scott Road. (photos by Helen Hegener/Northern Light Media.) Above: Sjodin barn, November 2008 (Photo: Stewart Amgwert)

Sjodin / Klem / Sojka
Scott Road, Palmer

Clarence and Alice Sjodin came from Onamia, Minnesota with two children and settled on tract number 98, a choice location bordered on the south side by Scott Road, about a mile northwest of Palmer. While the Sjodins left the Colony after a few years, their barn, with its classic lines of the standard Colony barn left mostly unaltered, has become a photogenic local landmark.

The description of the Sjodin barn published in the booklet, *Evaluation of Historic Sites in Palmer, Alaska*, printed in 1988 by the Matanuska-Susitna Borough Division of Cultural Resources, gives a few interesting details: "The barn is the standard gambrel colony barn. First floor walls are three-sided logs, vertical planks form the pony wall and the hay loft is covered with horizontal planks. A central cupola surmounts the roof. A large open trellis has been attached to the west side of the barn."

The 1940 U.S. Census records show the Sjodin family still on tract number 98, with five children ages 4, 5, and 6, and twins age one year old. Clarence's widowed father, Magnus, was also living with the family, and according the the census report he helped work on the family farm.

In James H. Fox's book, *The First Summer* (A.R.R.C., 1980) there are photos of Clarence Sjodin helping build the Joseph Puhl log home, and of Alice Sjodin doing laundry on the gas-powered washing machine which the Sjodins brought with them from Minnesota.

The *Historic Sites* book also described "assorted log outbuildings and corrals" on the property, and noted, "All utilize round logs and exhibit tight joinery and very good workmanship. Both lap notching and saddle notching is exhibited...." ~•~

THE MATANUSKA COLONY BARNS

Ising / Dragseth / Venne / Grover

Left: Beneath Byers Peak and Lazy Mountain to the east, the Dragseth (silver roof) and Ising (red roof) barns are to the right of the lone Venne barn on Wes Grover's RG Farm. (Photo by Helen Hegener/Northern Light Media). **Above: Detail of the three-sided spruce logs on the Venne barn. Facing page: The George Venne barn** (both photos by Eric Vercammen/Northern Light Media).

Ising/Dragseth/Venne/Grover
Grover Lane, Palmer

In October, 1914 Palmer pioneer John August Springer filed for homestead rights to 320 acres of benchland located on the north bank of a sweeping bend in the Matanuska River, with a commanding view of Pioneer Peak. Springer received the patent in 1920, and in 1935 he sold part of his homestead to the U.S. Government for $7.50 an acre for the Matanuska Colony Project.

William and Marie Ising and their two children joined the Matanuksa Colony Project from Saginaw, Minnesota. William drew tract number 81, one of the few 80 acre parcels, once part of John Springer's homestead.

In 1948, Clifton and Vera Grover, who had recently arrived in Alaska from Utah, bought the Ising Colony farm. According to their son, Wesley R Grover, who was 14 years old when they purchased the farm, the deal "...included about 15 cows, a Farmall H tractor, a big black horse and all the farm machinery we needed to get started and enjoy the fruits of our labor in the beautiful Matanuska Valley."

In 1962 John Springer died, and 70 acres adjoining the original Ising farm became available and was purchased by the Grover family for their growing dairy. Wes Grover and his wife Bonnie purchased the entire farm from his father in 1965, and after deciding not to continue the dairy business they leased the land to the Alaska Rodeo Association as pasture.

Over the years two additional Colony barns were moved onto the property, the Joseph Dragseth barn from tract number 84 was moved into place adjacent to the original Ising barn, and the George Venne barn from tract number 82 was set in a pasture just to the north of the other two barns.

The picturesque RG Farm, located at the end of Grover Lane, has been the location for many weddings, television commercials, and has been featured on the cover of the MTA phonebook. ~•~

THE MATANUSKA COLONY BARNS

THE MATANUSKA COLONY BARNS

110

THE MATANUSKA COLONY BARNS

"The picturesque RG Farm at the end of Grover Lane . . ."

Left: The George Venne barn. Above: weathervane on the Venne barn. (Photos by Eric Vercammen/Northern Light Media). **Upper right: The Venne barn. Lower right: Pioneer Peak looms over Wes Grover's RG Farm.** (Helen Hegener/Northern Light Media) **Lower left: Tools on the side of the George Venne barn.** (Eric Vercammen/Northern Light Media)

THE MATANUSKA COLONY BARNS

Patten / Gorman

Patten barns and silos, the barn is believed to be the only remaining original stallion barn. (Photo on the left by Stewart Amgwert, photos above and on the facing page by Helen Hegener/Northern Light Media)

Patten / Gorman
Mile 39.9 Glenn Highway, Palmer

The Patten family, Clair, Margaret, and their young daughter, joined the Colony project from Long Siding, Minnesota, and they drew tract no. 49, located just southeast of what would become the town of Palmer. Today the Patten farm, still owned by the family, sits just west of the state fairgrounds, alongside the Glenn Highway.

Excerpts from the 1998 *Evaluation of Historic Sites in Palmer* book: "The original Patten barn is unique among the colony structures. This barn is smaller than the typical colony barn and was built specifically to house one of three thoroughbred draft stallions owned by the ARRC. The Pattens and the Nelson family were selected to care for these expensive breeding horses-- only two barns of this type were known to have existed. The Patten stallion barn is believed to be the only example remaining.

"In 1936 the barn was extended, almost doubling its size and the new addition was used as a hay shed. The barn is now a large rectangular structure with a long, low gambrel roof.

"The largest barn is not original to the property. The Pattens purchased the Thomas Snyder tract in the early 1940's and relocated the barn to its present site. The Pattens began their dairy business in the early 1940's; their herd grew to 40 head and a milk house and milking stalls were added. The concrete silos, identical to those on the Rebarchek farm and constructed by Patten and Rebarchek, were built after the dairy business began.

"The Pattens sold their cows and quit the dairy business in 1968. The family has since used the barns and outbuildings for storage and leased the surrounding lands for haying."

With its many ancillary buildings, the Patten farm was noted in the *Evaluation of Historic Sites* as "an excellent representation of the complete Colony complex." ~•~

THE MATANUSKA COLONY BARNS

Barry / Hecker / Gardner

Left, circa 1936-37, shortly after the barn was completed for the Earl Barry family, who drew tract #140. Opposite page: The barn was owned by Earl and Kathreen Hecker in 1945. Above: After 1948 the barn was owned by their son, William Hecker. These three photos are used courtesy of Barbara Hecker, of Palmer. (Original photographers unknown)

Barry / Hecker / Gardner
North Campbell Road, Palmer

The Colony house and barn on Tract #140, on Campbell Road, just off the Palmer Fishhook Road north of Palmer, was originally owned by the Earl Barry family. The land, however, did not have enough tillable acreage, and the four-bedroom house was too small for the large Barry family, so the Barrys left the Colony to be on their own, and bought Bogard's homestead on Finger Lake.

In the early 1940s the farm was purchased by Earl and Kathreen Hecker. In 1948 their son William Hecker and his wife Bergie took over the farm and raised three daughters.

In 1989 Dr. Vaughn and Karen Gardner purchased the house, barn, and a large portion of the original homestead, and in the summer of 2012 the barn was restored. Local historian Barbara Hecker, who grew up on Tract #140 and still lives nearby, wrote an article about the barn's restoration for The Mat-Su Valley Frontiersman (Sept. 15, 2012), in which she noted, "My dad maintained the barn conscientiously. Colony barns were built on small pilings of native spruce. He lifted the barn and laid a foundation of 4-foot concrete pillars. He replaced the tarpaper roof with strong trusses and metal roofing. To weatherproof exterior log walls, he plastered stucco over chicken wire. Once a new Grade-A milking parlor was built in the early 1960s, the old red barn sheltered calves and heifers. In 24 years under Dr. Vaughn and Karen Gardner's guardianship, the barn has provided cover for sheep, llamas and alpacas."

As Barbara explained in her article, the restoration of the old barn came about through unusual circumstances. Dr. Gardner, an orthopedic surgeon, had a young patient with a particularly challenging broken leg, and it turned

THE MATANUSKA COLONY BARNS

115

THE MATANUSKA COLONY BARNS

"A deal was struck, and the boy's leg was well-mended..."

Left: The Hecker barn, mid-1980s (photo by Dave Rose). **Above: Hecker barn, circa 1970** (photo courtesy Barbara Hecker). **Opposite page: Gardner barn after the 2012 restoration** (photo by Barbara Hecker)

out that the young man's father was a fifth-generation barn rebuilder from Michigan. A deal was struck, the boy's leg was well mended, and the Mike Stitt family began work on the restoration of the barn. Barbara Hecker continues the story:

"For eight weeks, Stitt and his family crew tended to the Hecker/Gardner barn as lovingly and meticulously as an art restoration team handling a deteriorating masterpiece.

"Stitt's workplace does not ring with the buzz and pings and twirls of pneumatic or battery-driven tools. His gear includes jacks, come-alongs, cables, saws, hand-hewn wooden mallets, two-man tongs, a hand adze and a drawknife — some that date to the mid-1860s. These tools require no electricity, but plenty of elbow grease.

"Stitt jacked up the barn to remove the old concrete pillars and built a new foundation of cement bricks with reinforcing steel — the only contribution by today's construction processes and materials that is an improvement over the original building methods.

"Jacks pushed the log walls six- to eight-inches back into place. Rebar braces the inside walls against future assaults of wind. Paint, chicken wire, stucco and bark were peeled away from logs, revealing an amazingly intricate design of meandering insect trails. The beautifully blond, undamaged logs were left bare but for a Perma-Chink wood stain and durable sealant.

A new concrete floor was poured. Upper timber walls were repaired and repainted. Original pane windows were removed, repaired, cleaned and repainted, and replaced. The haymow was reinforced with a new floor. Eaves were boxed in. The metal roof painted. Gardner's grand old barn has never been so beautiful — nor so prepared for another century of service and storm." ~•~

Stahler/Jensen/Bouwens/McCormick/Olson

Left: Barns after being moved to their present location. (photo by Helen Hegener/Northern Light Media) **Above: The Jensen barn sits on the right, the Stahler barn on the left.** (photo by Eric Vercammen/Northern Light Media)

Stahler / Jensen / Bouwens / McCormick / Olson
7200 E. Valley Circle, Wasilla

An article in the *Mat-Su Valley Frontiersman* on January 28, 2012 by Heather Resz described a new business which had recently opened: "On the inside, the newly remodeled Coho Family Medicine looks more like your grandmother's cozy living room than a doctor's office waiting room. From the outside, the office looks much like it did in 1935 when John Stahler built the barn."

John and Elizabeth Stahler were the only Colonists from Oklahoma, and they came to Alaska with six children. John drew tract number 206 in the lottery for parcels, a site located at the end of what is today's Campbell Road, north of Palmer. A frame house was built for the family, and the standard Colony barn was raised. The barn traveled through several owners, including Tom Moffitt and Wayne Bouwens, before it finally left the area where it had originally been built.

Doug Olson bought the barn and moved it to the current site in 2002 with the help of his then-partner, Mark Loomis. A Jan. 9, 2004 article in the *Frontierman* by Daniel Spoth, titled *"Valley Man Makes A Living Driving Dump Trucks and Saving Historic Buildings,"* explained, "Loomis has been saving historical buildings for over eight years now, but he has fostered a concern for historic Valley buildings since his father tore down a decaying Colony barn that had stood on his property for years. After rescuing a threatened barn across the street from his home, he became increasingly interested in saving structures around the Valley, and now hosts five barns and other buildings on his property..."

When Dr. Steve Parker moved his family to Palmer from Michigan in 2009, he remembered seeing the barn

"...didn't think there was much merit to the barn..."

Above: Jensen barn in the original location. (photo by Stewart Amgwert) Right: A porch has been added across the back of the barns, which sit on a concrete block basement. (photo by Eric Vercammen/Northern Light Media)

and thinking it would make a great home, and he eventually located both his medical practice clinic and his young family in the historic barn.

The second barn on the site was originally built for the Henry and Edna Jensen family, who came from Littlefork, Minnesota. Henry drew tract number 29, which was located at the end of present-day Jensen Road, on the south side of the Parks Highway, across from Mat-Su Regional Hospital.

In October, 2001, an article in the *Mat-Su Valley Frontiersman* explained how the Jensen barn had been abandoned to the elements and "...was scheduled to be burned as part of a training program for Mat-Su Borough firefighters..."

Upon learning that the owner of the Colony barn had donated it for the fire training exercise, Fran Seager-Boss of the borough's cultural resources division contacted Palmer Historical Society members, trying to find someone who might want to save the barn. She explained, "Typically the EMS does not burn down historical buildings. The owner didn't think there was much merit to the barn, but the community felt that it was one of the better preserved barns..."

Seager-Boss was directed to Doug Olson and Mark Loomis, who determined that the Jensen barn would survive a move and set about getting the huge structure ready.

The barn was moved to its present location at the end of Trunk Road, alongside the old Stahler barn. A cement block daylight basement runs the full length of both barns, providing additional living and storage space.

The Stahler and Jensen barns may not be in their final resting places yet. State highway plans include carving a road through the property on which they sit to provide easier access to a school a couple of miles away. Issues of public right-of-way and eminent domain are under discussion. ~•~

THE MATANUSKA COLONY BARNS

A Colony Barns Album

Smith barn, in original location on tract no. 65, at the end of McLeod Road off the Outer Springer Loop Road, south of Palmer. (Photo by Albert Marquez/Planet Earth Adventures)

THE MATANUSKA COLONY BARNS

Gulberg barn on tract 110, at Mile 52 of the Glenn Highway. (Photo by Helen Hegener/Northern Light Media)

THE MATANUSKA COLONY BARNS

The Oscar Kerttula barn, built on tract number 134 near the intersection of the Glenn Highway and Fishhook Road, collapsed in 2006. (Photo by Dave Rose)

THE MATANUSKA COLONY BARNS

The Vasanoja/Lebing/Kalwies barn, which was on tract no. 79, on Kalwies Road, off the Springer Loop System south of Palmer, finally collapsed in the fall of 2011. (Photo by Helen Hegener/Northern Light Media)

THE MATANUSKA COLONY BARNS

The Greise-Kalwies barn on Springer Loop Road, tract no. 77, south of Palmer. (Photo by Stewart Amgwert)

Unusual barrel vault roofed Arndt/Swift barn on tract no. 190, alongside the present-day Palmer-Wasilla Highway. (Photo: Helen Hegener/Northern Light Media)

Originally built for the Lloyd Bell family on tract number 194, this barn later belonged to Doc McKenzie, a local dentist. Located at Doc McKenzie Road and Bodenburg Loop. (Photo by Helen Hegener/Northern Light Media)

THE MATANUSKA COLONY BARNS

The Glendon Doughty barn is located on original tract no. 63, on McLeod Road, off the southern end of Outer Springer Loop Road. (Photo by Albert Marquez/Planet Earth Adventures)

THE MATANUSKA COLONY BARNS

The Virgil Eckert barn, one of the few barrel vault roofed barns, has been transformed into a home. It is on the original tract number 100, just south of Scott Road and the Glenn Highway. (photo by Stewart Amgwert)

THE MATANUSKA COLONY BARNS

Pioneer Peak and the DePriests' Tiny Moose Farm on Outer Springer Loop Road, south of Palmer.
(photo by Helen Hegener/Northern Light Media)

The Matanuska Colony Families

1. Alexander, H. (tract no. 9)
2. Anderson, C. (tract no. 113)
3. Anderson, Cl. (tract no. 121)
4. Anderson, W.
5. Archer, P. (tract no. 193)
6. Arndt, L. (tract no. 190)
7. Bailey, F. (tract no. 152)
8. Barry, E. (tract no. 140)
9. Bell, L. (tract no. 194)
10. Bennett, W. (tract no. 68)
11. Benson, H. (tract no. 95)
12. Bergan, L. (tract no. 181)
13. Beylund, O. (tract no. 94)
14. Biller, R.
15. Boice, H. (tract no. 1)
16. Bouwens, W. (tract no. 53)
17. Bradley, J.
18. Brown, O.
19. Campbell, G. (tract no. 54)
20. Campbell, H. (tract no. 138)
21. Carson, A. (tract no. 13)
22. Carter, C.
23. Casler, W. (tract no. 38)
24. Chaney, E.
25. Christianson, M.
26. Church, J. (tract no. 26)
27. Clayton, W. (tract no. 48)
28. Connors, G. (tract no. 132)
29. Cook, C.
30. Cousineau, C.
31. Covert, A.
32. Davis, H. (tract no. 127)
33. Dean, B. (tract no. 159)
34. Deland, N. (tract no. 136)
35. Dingman, W.
36. Doughty, G. (tract no. 63)
37. Dragseth, J. (tract no. 84)
38. Dreghorn, L. (tract no. 175)
39. Durfey, R.
40. Eckert, V. (tract no. 100)
41. Ellison, C. (tract no. 200)
42. Ellsworth, L. (tract no. 191)
43. Emberg, G.
44. Engebretson, O.
45. Ennes, M. (tract no. 149)
46. Erickson, C. (tract no. 58)
47. Ferguson, W. (tract no. 42)
48. Fisher, O.
49. Fitzpatrick, T.
50. Foster, K. (tract no. 85)
51. Fox, W. (tract no. 89)
52. France, G. (tract no. 16)
53. Frank, D. (tract no. 187)
54. Frederick, A.
55. Fredericks, A. (tract no. 87)
56. Giblin, T.
57. Greene, C.
58. Griese, R. (tract no. 77)
59. Gulberg, B. (tract no. 110)
60. Hack, A.
61. Hamann, L. (tract no. 108)
62. Havemeister, A. (trt no. 167)
63. Hemmer, P. (tract no. 44)
64. Henry, F. (tract no. 104)
65. Hermon, J. (tract no. 43)
66. Herried, L. (tract no. 139)
67. Hess, F.
68. Hesse, C. (tract no. 101)
69. Higgenbotham, R. (trt 202)
70. Hoeft, J.
71. Hoganson, H. (tract no. 71)
72. Holler, J.
73. Hopkins, R.
74. Huntley, W. (tract no. 80)
75. Huseby, E. (tract no. 34)
76. Hynek, W. (tract no. 91)
77. Ising, W. (tract no. 81)
78. Jacobsen, A. (tract no. 45)
79. Jahr, P.
80. Jensen, Harry (tract no. 173)
81. Jensen, Henry (tract no. 29)
82. Johnson, A. (tract no. 169)
83. Johnson, C. (tract no. 105)
84. Johnson, H. (tract no. 153)
85. Johnson, J. (tract no. 15)
86. Johnson, V. (tract no. 97)
87. Johnston, J. (tract no. 22)
88. Jones, V. (tract no. 144)
89. Juvette, E. (tract no. 8)
90. Kalliosaari, J.
91. Kenser, G. (tract no. 96)
92. Kerttula, O. (tract no. 134)
93. Kindgren, O. (tract no. 170)
94. Kirsch, J. (tract no. 64)
95. Klinepier, K. (tract no. 158)
96. Koenan, H.
97. Kurtz, C. (tract no. 51)
98. Laako, H. (tract no. 37)
99. LaFlam, C.
100. Lake, J. (tract no. 73)
101. La Rose, H. (tract no. 135)
102. Larsh, E. (tract no. 31)
103. Larson, F. (tract no. 24)
104. La Valley, E. (tract no. 18)
105. Leander, R.
106. Lee, F.S. (tract no. 207)
107. Lemmon, Geo.
108. Lemmon, Gil.
109. Lentz, J. (tract no. 183)
110. Lentz, Wm. (tract no. 133)
111. Lepak, T. (tract no. 90)
112. Lipke, H.
113. Loyer, J. (tract no. 62)
114. Lund, J.
115. MacNevin, L. (tract no. 60)
116. Manginen, W.
117. Martin, C.
118. Mattson, R. (tract no. 55)
119. McCormick, M.
120. McKechnie, L. (trt no. 199)
121. McKendry, H.
122. Meehan, J. (tract no. 56)
123. Meier, C. (tract no. 39)
124. Miller, N. (tract no. 155)
125. Monroe, L. (tract no. 185)
126. Moses, A.
127. Moss, E. (tract no. 30)
128. Nelson, A. (tract no. 27)
129. Nelson, P. (tract no. 178)
130. Newville, I. (tract no. 196)
131. Nichols, H.
132. Novak, G. (tract no. 57)
133. Nutilla, E. (tract no. 201)
134. Olmstead, V. (tract no. 28)
135. Olson, H.
136. Olson, W.
137. Onkka, D. (tract no. 61)
138. Pakonen, R.
139. Parks, C. (tract no. 189)
140. Parlette, P. (tract no. 131)
141. Patten, C. (tract no. 49)
142. Peterson, O. (tract no. 186)
143. Pfeiff, J. (tract no. 76)
144. Piaskowski, F. (trt no. 177)
145. Pippel, W. (tract no. 106)
146. Poor, C.
147. Poore, M. (tract no. 41)
148. Porter, J. (tract no. 124)
149. Porterfield, E.
150. Powell, O.
151. Puhl, J. (tract no. 99)
152. Quarnstrom, C. (tr no. 114)
153. Raschke, A.
154. Rebarchek, R. (tract no. 52)
155. Reitan, B. (tract no. 75)
156. Retallic, A.
157. Ring, F. (tract no. 93)
158. Rorrison, L. (tract no. 112)
159. Rossiter, H.
160. Rotz, F. (tract no. 92)
161. Roughan, H.
162. Ruddell, C. (tract no. 17)
163. Runyon, S.
164. Saarela, M.
165. Sandvik, I. (tract no. 47)
166. Scheibl, G. (tract no. 59)
167. Schultz, W.
168. Schutt, C.
169. Sexton, A. (tract no. 11)
170. Sieber, J. (tract no. 182)
171. Sjodin, C. (tract no. 98)
172. Smith, L. (tract no. 180)
173. Smith, M.
174. Smith, W. (tract no. 65)
175. Snyder, T. (tract no. 50)
176. Sorenson, C. (tract no. 86)
177. Soyk. M. (tract no. 107)
178. Spencer, M.
179. Splittgerber, H.
180. Stahler, J. (tract no. 206)
181. Stebbins, D. (tract no. 122)
182. Stephen, V. (tract no. 179)
183. Strang, E.
184. Sturdy, N. (tract no. 72)
185. Sullivan, C. (tract no. 88)
186. Swanda, F. (tract no. 70)
187. Taylor, N.
188. Uber, L. (tract no. 160)
189. Usher, R.
190. VanWormer, H. (tr no. 198)
191. Vasanoja, L. (tract no. 79)
192. Venne, G. (tract no. 82)
193. Vickaryous, A. (tract no. 4)
194. Walport, P.
195. Way, S.
196. Weiler, N. (tract no. 2)
197. Wilding, J.
198. Wilkes, R.
199. Wilson, A. (tract no. 32)
200. Wirtanen, E. (tract no. 143)
201. Worden, F. (tract no. 10)
202. Yohn, V. (tract no. 168)
203. Zook, H. (tract no. 205)

CREDIT: PAUL HILL, JUSTER HILL PRODUCTIONS

The Matanuska Colony Tract Maps

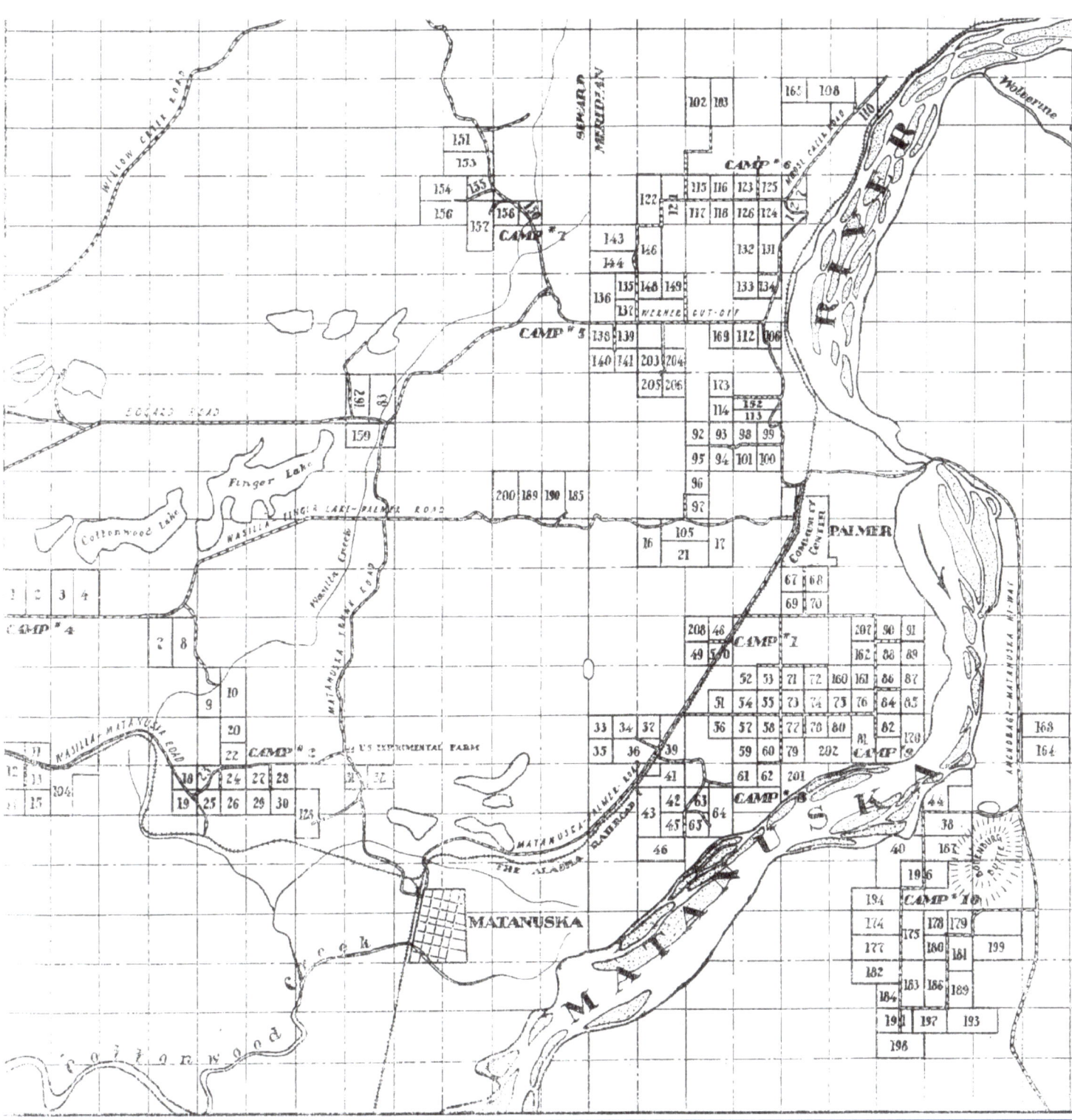

OVERVIEW • DETAILED MAPS ON FOLLOWING PAGES

THE MATANUSKA COLONY BARNS

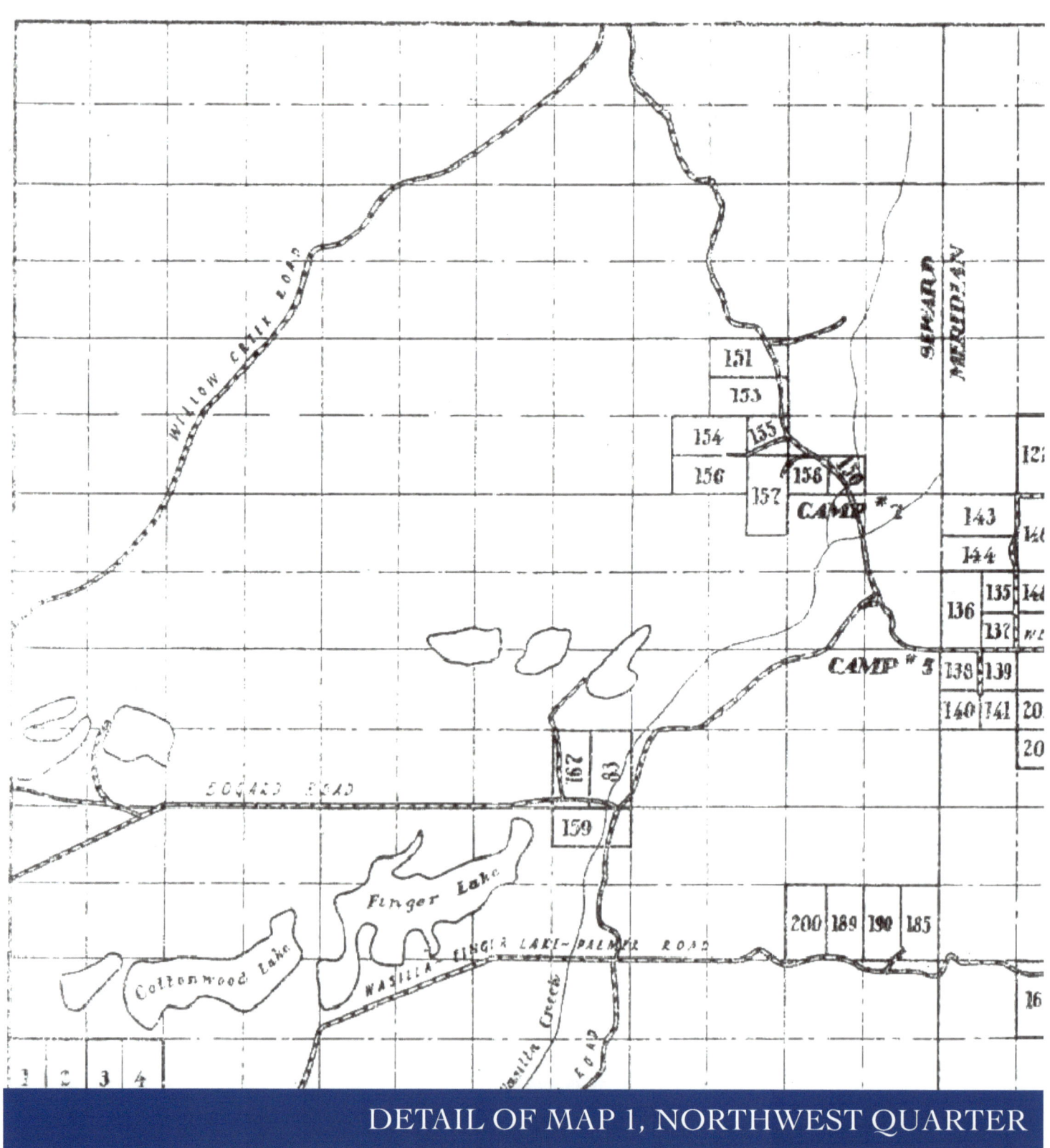

DETAIL OF MAP 1, NORTHWEST QUARTER

THE MATANUSKA COLONY BARNS

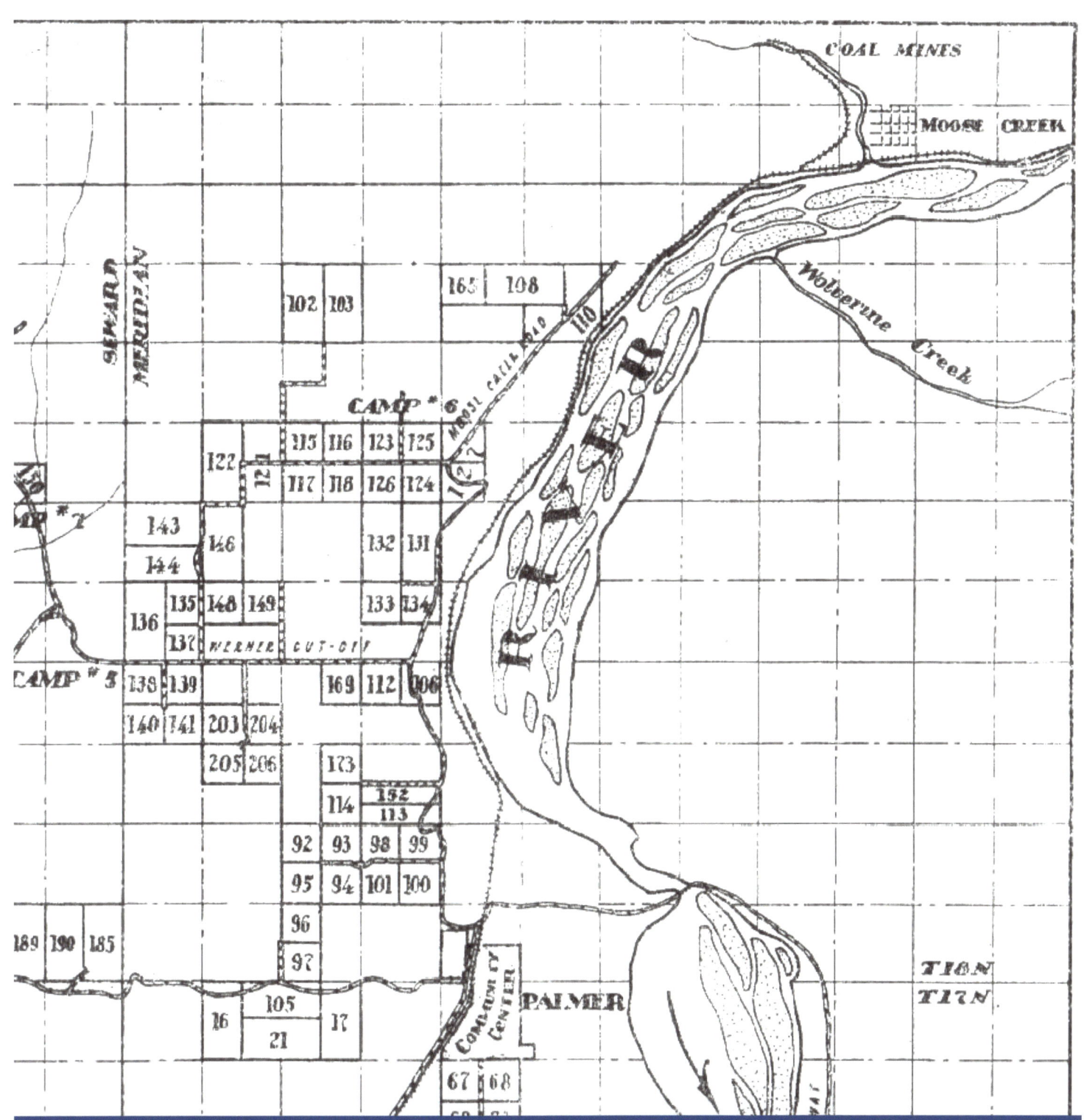

DETAIL OF MAP 1, NORTHEAST QUARTER

THE MATANUSKA COLONY BARNS

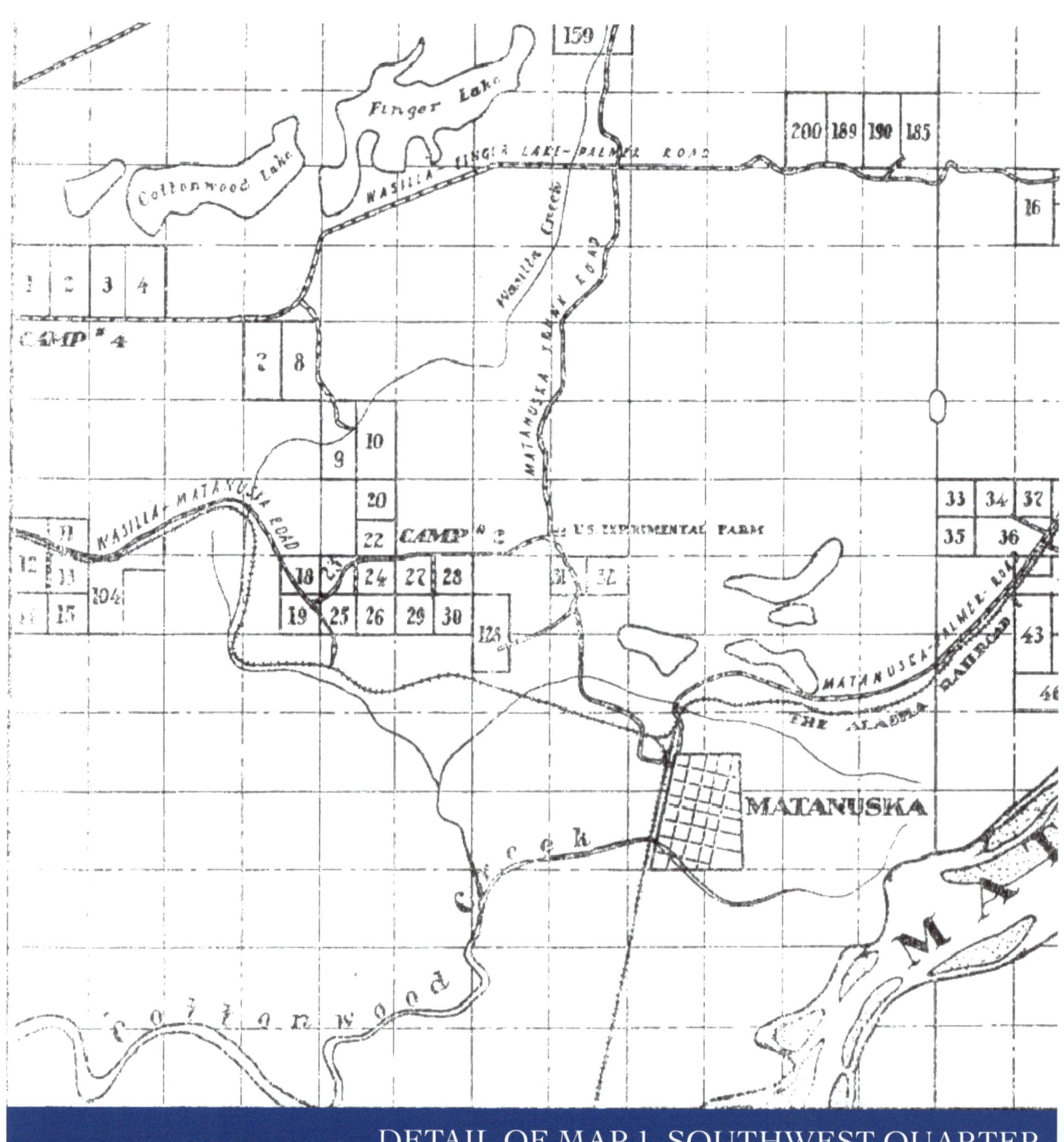

DETAIL OF MAP 1, SOUTHWEST QUARTER

THE MATANUSKA COLONY BARNS

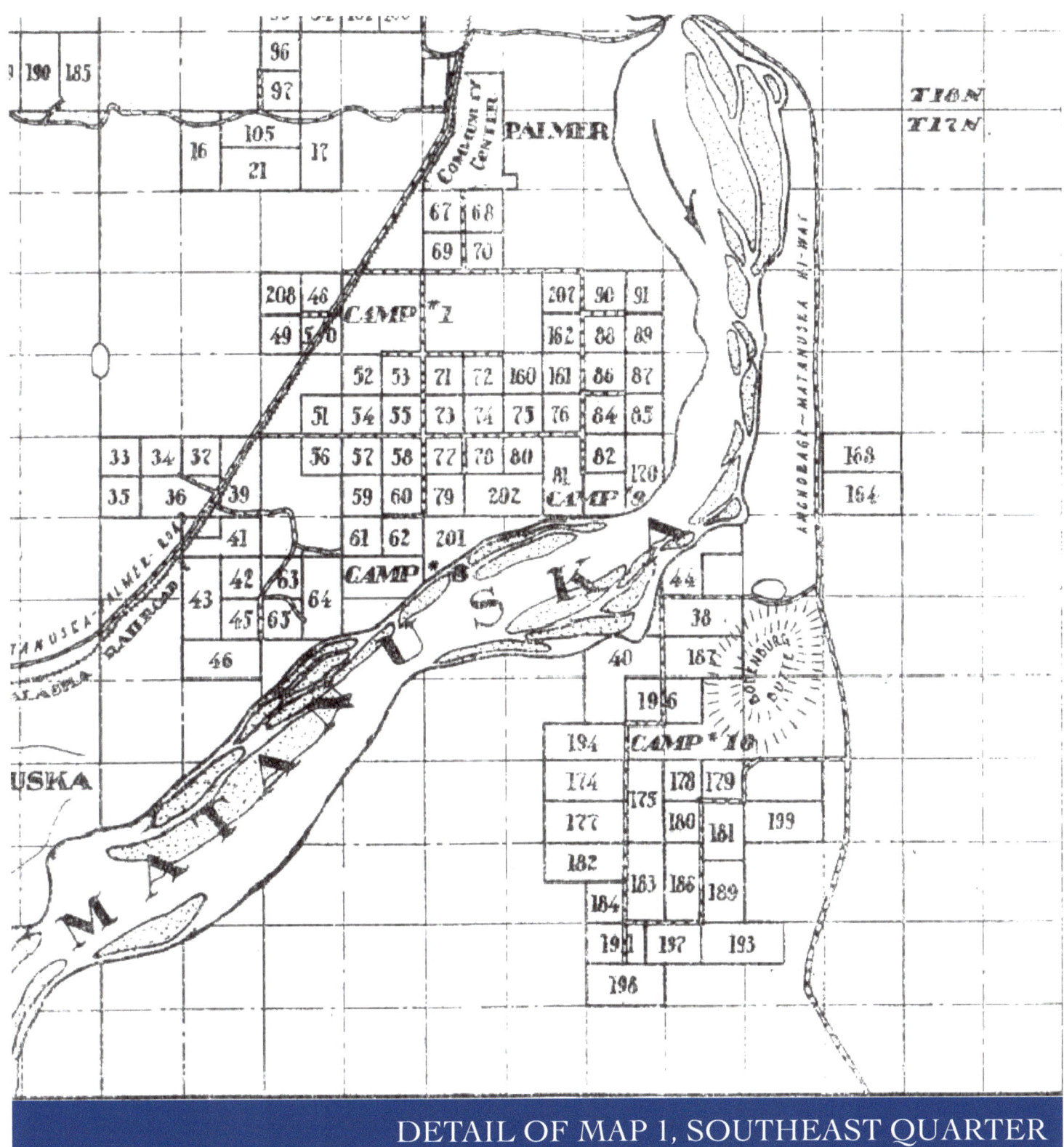

DETAIL OF MAP 1, SOUTHEAST QUARTER

Bibliography • Resources

• Bibliography •

Atwood, Evangeline • *We Shall Be Remembered* (Anchorage: The Alaska Methodist University, 1966)

Fox, James H. • *The First Summer: Photographs of the Matanuska Colony of 1935* (A.R.R.C., 1980)

Hoagland, Alison K. • *Buildings of Alaska* (New York: Oxford University Press, 1993)

Irwin, Don L. • *The Colorful Matanuska Valley* (1968)

Johnson, Hugh A. and Keith L. Stanton • *Matanuska Valley Memoir: The Story of How One Alaskan Community Developed* (Alaska Experiment Station, 1955)

Jordan, Nancy • *Frontier Physician: The Life and Legacy of Dr. C. Earl Albrecht* (Epicenter Press, 1995)

Kirker, Lorraine M. and Lynette A. Lehn • *Matanuska Colony 75th Anniversary Scrapbook* (Alaskana Books, 2010)

Lively, Brigitte • *The Matanuska Colony: Fifty Years: 1935-1985* (Matanuska Impressions Printing, 1985)

Lively, Brigette • *Matanuska Colony Sixty Years: 1935-1995: The Colonists and Their Legacy* (ARRC, 1985)

Matanuska-Susitna Borough • *Evaluation of Historic Sites in Palmer, Alaska* (Matanuska-Susitna Borough Cultural Resources Division, 1988)

Matanuska-Susitna Borough • *Knik, Matanuska, Susitna: A Visual History of the Valleys* (L & B Color Printing, 1985)

Miller, Orlando W. • *The Frontier in Alaska and the Matanuska Colony* (Yale University Press, 1975)

Potter, Louise • *A Study of a Frontier Town in Alaska: Wasilla to 1959* (Hanover, 1963)

Potter, Louise • *Old Times on Upper Cook's Inlet* (The Book Cache, 1967)

Rebarcheck, Raymond • *Memoirs of an Alaskan Farmer* (Vantage Press, 1980)

• Resources & References •

Agroborealis Magazine, November 1972; UAF School of Natural Resources & Agricultural Sciences, Fairbanks, AK
http://www.uaf.edu/snras/publications/agroborealis/

Alaskana Books
564 S. Denali St., Palmer, AK 99645
1-888-354-9483
www.alaskanabooks.com/

Alaska Dispatch
Farmer Arthur Keyes is restoring a 1930s barn on his property near Palmer. Feb. 3, 2011. Stephen Nowers photos. http://www.alaskadispatch.com/slideshow/restoring-colony-barn

Alaska Far Away: The New Deal Pioneers of the Matanuska Valley. DVD by Paul Hill & Joanie Juster (Juster Hill Productions, 2008)
www.alaskafaraway.com

Alaska's Digital Archives
http://vilda.alaska.edu/

Alaska Farmland Trust
http://www.akfarmland.com/

Alaska's Timeline
http://www.litsite.org/aktimeline/

Alaska Trails to the Past
Matanuska Valley Project
http://alaskaweb.org/mvc.html

Anchorage Press News
Heaven's Ghost Town, by Scott Christiansen; December 16, 2009
http://www.anchoragepress.com/news/heaven-s-ghost-town/article_27e35ff5-f15d-5a08-8d4a-b83a8123d2a2.html

Brooks Fairview Loop Survey
http://www.brooks-alaska.com/fairviewloop/documents/05_51774_FairviewLpCRSurvey_Arch&BuiltEnv.pdf

Federal Rural Development Policy in the Twentieth Century
Dennis Roth, Anne B. W. Effland, Douglas E. Bowers; United States Department of Agriculture - Economic Research Service; 2002 Links modified July, 2008
www.nal.usda.gov/ric/ricpubs/rural_development_policy.html

LitSite Alaska
http://www.litsite.org/

Mary Nan Gamble Collection
University of Alaska Fairbanks
http://cdm1.library.uaf.edu/cdm/compoundobject/collection/cdmg21/id/4336/rec/1

THE MATANUSKA COLONY BARNS

Matanuska Susitna Valley, Alaska Learning about Our Earliest Residents A history and geneology web site by Colleen Mielke
freepages.genealogy.rootsweb.ancestry.com/~coleen/matanuska_susitna.html

Matanuska Valley Pioneer Directory by Colleen Mielke
freepages.genealogy.rootsweb.ancestry.com/~coleen/wasilla_pioneer_directory.html

Mat-Su Valley Frontiersman
Born to Raise Barn, by JJ Harrier, July 10, 2007
http://www.frontiersman.com/news/born-to-raise-barn/article_e043063a-75fd-56a7-9e01-f36a008e9815.html

Mat-Su Valley Frontiersman
Breeden Barn Moves, by *Frontiersman* news staff, Aug. 28, 2007
http://www.frontiersman.com/news/breeden-barn-moves/article_d498410b-d887-5da8-85e3-6b4246de8c2e.html

Mat-Su Valley Frontiersman
Fire training at Colony barn halted, by Scott Christiansen, October 23, 2001
http://www.frontiersman.com/fire-training-at-colony-barn-halted/article_023c1662-5e51-5f74-939a-8a3f32135f69.html

Mat-Su Valley Frontiersman
Old barn is new 'Coho Family Medicine,' by Heather A. Resz, Saturday, January 28, 2012
http://www.frontiersman.com/business/old-barn-is-new-coho-family-medicine/article_71e8db2e-4a4b-11e1-bfa3-001871e3ce6c.html

Mat-Su Valley Frontiersman
Past more simple, but not necessarily better, by Greg Johnson, Dec. 26, 2010
frontiersman.com/news/past-more-simple-but-not-necessarily-better/article_c72db3e6-6bcf-5326-889e-9e4dad917783.html

Mat-Su Valley Frontiersman
Historic structure ready to face another century of Valley life, by Barbara Hecker, Sept. 15, 2012
http://www.frontiersman.com/valley_life/historic-structure-ready-to-face-another-century-of-valley-life/article_9101203c-ffb0-11e1-b853-001a4bcf887a.html

Museum of Alaska Transportation & Industry (MATI)
3800 W. Museum Dr., Wasilla, AK, 99654 (907) 376-1211
www.museumofalaska.org/

New Deal Preservation Association
Kathy Flynn, Ex. Director, PO Box 602, Santa Fe, NM 87504. (505) 473.3985
http://newdeallegacy.org/index.html

Palmer Historical Society
316 E. Elmwood Avenue, Palmer, AK 99645 (907) 745-1935
www.palmerhistoricalsociety.org/

Rondayview Photography
I Visit The Alaska Transportation Museum & Breeden Barn; Posted on March 31, 2010 by Ron Day
http://rondayvous.com/blog1/2010/03/31/i-visit-the-alaska-transportation-museum-breeden-barn/

Palmer Museum and Visitor Center
723 South Valley Way
Palmer, AK 99645
Phone: (907) 746-7668
www.palmermuseum.org/

Stewart Amgwert's Colony barns collection: http://nopeople.com/homepage/Colony%20Barns/index.html

The Matanuska Colony: The New Deal in Alaska
A web site by Murray Lundberg
http://explorenorth.com/library/yafeatures/bl-matanuska.htm

U.S. National Archives and Records Administration
654 W 3rd Ave, Anchorage, AK 99501
Phone: (907) 261-7820
www.archives.gov/anchorage/

Wasilla Pioneers Directory
freepages.genealogy.rootsweb.ancestry.com/~coleen/wasilla_pioneer_directory.html

Waymarking Palmer, Alaska
http://www.waymarking.com/waymarks/WM9H4M_Matanuska_Colony_Project_Palmer_Alaska

Where the River Matanuska Flows: Stories from Alaska Pioneers
DVD by Paul Hill & Joanie Juster (Juster Hill Productions, 2008)
www.alaskafaraway.com

Please advise the author of any errors or omissions in this listing and changes will be made to the next edition of this book:
helenhegener@gmail.com

Barns Index & Locations Map

Barns are listed by original Colonists' names only. Page numbers are in parentheses.

1. Doughty (1, 63, 127)
2. Venne (2, 8, 10, 54, 55, 108-111)
3. Sjodin (3, 5, 106-107)
4. Parks-Archer (6, 96-99)
5. Smith (7, 120)
6. J. Lentz (7, 54, 62,
7. Havemeister (7, 9, 80-81)
8. Arndt (7, 100-101, 125)
9. Barry (11, 114-117)
10. Patten (12, 112-113)
11. Benson (12)
12. Kerttula (14, 122)
13. Vanderweele (15)
14. Rebarchek (51, 104-105 *orig. location*)
15. Bailey (64-67)
16. Wilson-Larsh (50, 68-71 *orig. location*)
17. Puhl (72-75)
18. Loyer-Lake (76-79)
19. Anderson (82-83)
20. Johnson (84-87 *orig. location*)
21. Wm. Lentz (88-89)
22. Wineck (90-95 *orig. location*)
23. Monroe (102-103)
24. Ising-Dregseth (108-111)
25. Stahler-Jenson (118-119)
26. Gulberg (121)
27. Vasanoja (123)
28. Griese (124)
29. Bell (126)
30. Eckert (128)
31. DePriest (129)
32. Bergan (51)
33. Carson (51)

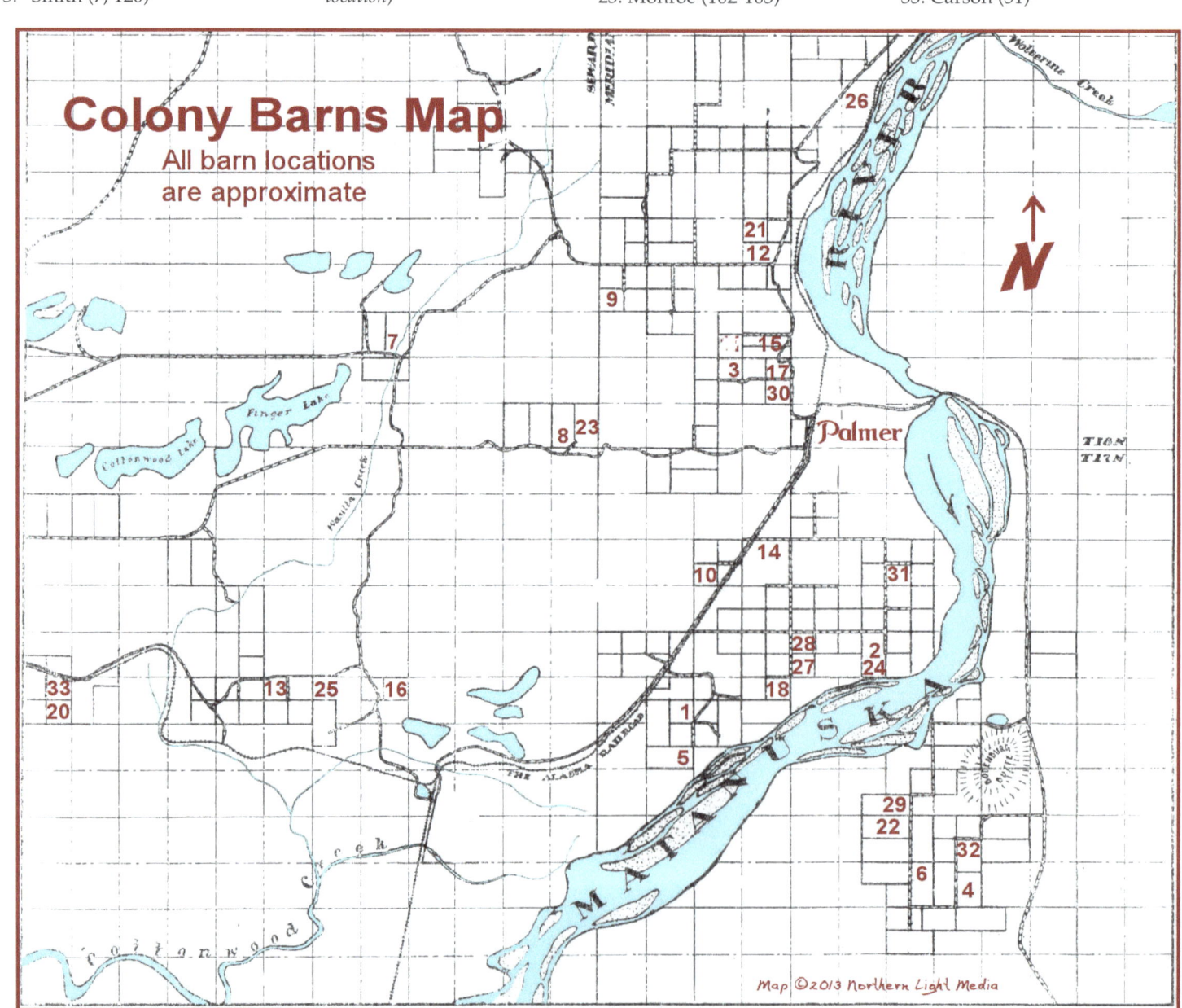

/ THE MATANUSKA COLONY BARNS

Index

AEC Headquarters barn 24
agriculture 37, 38, 40, 44, 48
Alaska Far Away 10, 136
Alaska Railroad 24, 34, 44
Alaska State Fair 80, 90-95, 105
Anderson, Anton 52
appraisal, barn 60
arched roof 73, 101, 102
Archer, Floyd **(barn)** 96-99
Archer, Glen 96
Archer, Perle **(barn)** 96
architect, Colony 45, 51, 52, 53
Arndt, Lawrence **(barn)** 100-101, 125
Arthurdale, West Virginia 43
Bacon barn 72-75
Bacon, Dexter **(barn) 72-75**
Bailey, Ferber **(barn)** 60-65
barn restoration 116-119
barn, stallion 53
barns, blueprint 56
barns, complaints 47, 56, 59
barns, construction 50-53, 56, 59
barns, cost 59
barns, design 53, 56, 59
barns, double 69
barns, moved 65, 69, 70, 73, 114, 118-119
barns, problems 47, 56, 59
barns, size 47
barrel vault roof 73, 101, 102
Barry, Earl **(barn)** 48, 114-117
Bell, Lloyd **(barn)** 126
Benson, Henning **(barn)** 12
Bouwens, Wayne **(barn)** 118-119
Breeden, Don & LaVera **(barn)** 9, 50, 69
Campbell, George **(barn)** 59, 60
Carson, Arnold **(barn)** 51
Church, Edward 101
Colony tract maps 131-135
Creamer's Dairy barn 27
dog barn 23
Doughty, Glendon **(barn)** 1, 125
Dragseth, Joseph **(barn)** 108-111
Dyess Colony, Arkansas 43
Eckert, Virgil **(barn)** 73, 101, 102, 128
Estelle, Richard **(barn)** 65
Fairbanks Experimnt Station 40
Fox, James H. 10, 12, 96, 136

Frontiersman 70, 80, 116, 120-121
Fuller, S.R. 53
Gardner, Dr. Vaughn & Karen **(barn)** 11, 114-117
Gislason, Joe & Myrtle 84
Great Depression 43, 51
Greise, Raymond **(barn)** 126
Grover, Clifton **(barn)** 9, 10, 54, 55, 108-111
Grover, Wes & Bonnie 54, 55, 108-111
Gulberg, Bernard **(barn)** 121
Hatch Act 28
Havemeister, Arnold **(barn)** 9, 80-81
Havemeister, Bob & Jeanne 80
Heady, J. 37
Heaven, Leroi & Margaret **(barn)** 9, 10, 51, 84-87
Hecker, Barbara 10, 11, 114-117
Hecker, Earl **(barn)** 11, 114-117
Hecker, William & Bergie **(barn)** 11, 114-117
Hinckley, Charles 27
Hoagland, Alison K. 23, 24, 40
homesteaders, early 37, 40
Hunt, Colonel 52
Huseby, E.H. 45
Irwin, Don L. 43, 44
Ising, William **(barn)** 108-111
James Taylor dog barn 23
Jensen, Henry **(barn)** 60,118-119
Johnson, Hugh 37, 40, 47, 56, 59
Johnson, Johan **(barn)** 45, 84
Juster, Joanie 10, 136
Kalwies **(barn)** 125, 126
Kerttula, Oscar **(barn)** 14, 122
Keyes, Arthur **(barn)** 105-106
Kinty, Glenn & Rollo 101
Kircher, Joe 38
Klem barn 108-109
Knik 34, 37
Krough, Oliver 38
Laing, Kathy (Roark) 101, 102
Lake, John **(barn)** 76-79
Lamb, Shane 77, 79
Larsh, Emil **(barn)** 69
Lebing barn 125
Lentz, Joseph **(barn)** 88-89
Lentz, William **(barn)** 88
Linn, Allen 69

Linn, Frank **(barn)** 9, 50, 60, 69
Loomis, Mark 120-121
Loyer, Dottie, Rita **(barn)** 76-79
Luster **(barn)** 83
Mat-Su Valley Frontiersman 70, 80, 116, 118-119
Matanuska Colony Historic District 53
Matanuska Colony Project 43
Matanuska Experiment Station 28, 37, 69
Matanuska Junction 38, 43
Matanuska River 9, 17, 20, 21,34
Matanuska Valley 17, 18, 21
Mattson, Runar **(barn)** 105-106
McCombs, Bob **(barn)** 84
McKenzie, Doc **(barn)** 126
Miller, Neil 74
Miller, Orlando W. 18
Mitchell, Lt. Wm. "Billy" 23
Monroe, Lester **(barn)** 102-103
Mucks, Arlie 45
Museum of Alaska Trans. & Industry 68-70
Musk Ox Farm **(barn)** 88-89
National Register of Historic Places 28, 53, 60, 65, 73
Nelson family 114
Nelson, Margaret 43
Olson, Doug **(barn)** 60, 118-119
Palmer depot 34
Palmer Historical Society 119
Palmer, G.W. 34
Parker, Dr. Steve 118-119
Parks, Donald **(barn)** 96-99
Parsons, Captain 52
Patten, Clair **(barn)** 60,112-113
Peterson, Otto **(barn)** 99
Phoenix Homesteads, AZ 43
Pippel, Walter **(barn)** 48, 60, 73
Post, Lillian 99
Potter, Louise 34, 37
Puhl, Joseph **(barn)** 72-75, 101, 102
Puhl, Raymond 74
Raven's Roost **(barn)** 83
Rebarchek, Raymond **(barn)** 51, 60, 104-105
Riley, Helen 80
Roach, Cappy **(barn)** 83
Roark, Bill **(barn)** 102-103

Roosevelt, Franklin D. 43, 52
Saindon, G.H. 34, 44
Sandvik, Lynn 96
Seager-Boss, Fran 48, 119
Sherrod, Max 105
Shortridge, James R. 38
Sjodin, Clarence **(barn)** 106-107
Sloane, Eric 48
Smith, William **(barn)** 122
Snodgrass, M.D. 28
Snyder, Thomas **(barn)** 114
Sojka **(barn)** 108-109
Springer, John August 110
Stahler, John **(barn)** 60, 118-119
Stallion barn 53, 114-115
Stanton, Keith 37, 40, 47, 56, 59
Stevenson, Maureen **(barn)** 83
Stitt, Mike 116-119
Strong, Bonita Parks **(barn)** 96
Swanson, A.J. 84
Swift, Robert **(barn)** 101, 127
Taylor, James, dog barn 23
Tugwell, Rexford G. 28
Vanderweele-Keyes **(barn)** 15
Vasanoja, Lawrence **(barn)** 123
Venne, George **(barn)** 9, 10, 54, 55, 108-111
Vercammen, Eric 10
Vickaryous, Anthony **(barn)** 83
Vosburgh, John 83
Wasilla-Knik History Society 84
water tower, Palmer 60
Watson, D.F. 44
Weiss, Rudolf 38
White's farm 34
Wilson, Amadee **(barn)** 69
Wilson, Carl **(barn)** 74
Wineck, Earl **(barn)** 60, 90-95, 129
Wineck, Ed 60, 90-95, 129
Wineck, Uldrick 91

www.ingramcontent.com/pod-product-compliance
Lightning Source LLC
Chambersburg PA
CBHW041525220426
43670CB00002B/31